PHILADELPHIA, HERE I COME!

by the same author

PHILADELPHIA, HERE I COME!

BRIAN FRIEL

faber and faber
LONDON · BOSTON

First published in 1965
by Faber and Faber Limited
3 Queen Square London WCIN 3AU

ISBN 0 571 08586 5

For my Father and Mother

The first performance of *Philadelphia, Here I Come!* was given at the Gaiety Theatre, Dublin, on 28th September 1964 by Edwards-MacLiammoir: Dublin Gate Theatre Productions Ltd in association with the Dublin Theatre Festival and Oscar Lewenstein Ltd. It was directed by Hilton Edwards, and the setting was by Alpho O'Reilly. The cast was as follows:

MADGE		Maureen O'Sullivan
GARETH O'DONNELL {	*in Public*	Patrick Bedford
	in Private	Donal Donnelly
S. B. O'DONNELL		Éamonn Kelly
KATE DOOGAN		Máire Hastings
SENATOR DOOGAN		Cecil Barror
MASTER BOYLE		Dominic Roche
LIZZY SWEENEY		Ruby Head
CON SWEENEY		Tom Irwin
BEN BURTON		Michael Mara
NED		Éamon Morrissey
TOM		Brendan O'Sullivan
JOE		Emmet Bergin
CANON MICK O'BYRNE		Alex McDonald

Cast

Madge	*Housekeeper*
Gar O'Donnell (Public)	
Gar O'Donnell (Private)	*Son of the house*
S. B. O'Donnell	*Gar's father*
Kate Doogan/Mrs King	*Daughter of Senator Doogan*
Senator Doogan	
Master Boyle	*Local teacher*
Lizzy Sweeney	*Gar's aunt*
Con Sweeney	*Lizzy's husband*
Ben Burton	*Friend of the Sweeneys*
Ned	
Tom	*The boys*
Joe	
Canon Mick O'Byrne	*The parish priest*

*There is an interval at the end of Episode I and at the
end of Episode II*

Time: the present in the small village of Ballybeg in County Donegal, Ireland. The action takes place on the night before, and on the morning of, Gar's departure for Philadelphia.

When the curtain rises the only part of the stage that is lit is the kitchen, i.e. the portion on the left from the point of view of the audience. It is sparsely and comfortlessly furnished—a bachelor's kitchen. There are two doors; one left which leads to the shop, and one upstage leading to the scullery [off]. Beside the shop door is a large deal table, now set for tea without cloth and with rough cups and saucers. Beside the scullery door is an old-fashioned dresser. On the scullery wall is a large school-type clock.

Stage right, now in darkness, is Gar's bedroom. Both bedroom and kitchen should be moved upstage, leaving a generous apron. Gar's bedroom is furnished with a single bed, a wash-hand basin (crockery jug and bowl), a table with a record-player and records, and a small chest of drawers.

These two areas—kitchen and Gar's bedroom—occupy more than two-thirds of the stage. The remaining portion is fluid: in Episode I for example, it represents a room in Senator Doogan's home.

The two Gars, Public Gar and Private Gar, are two views of the one man. Public Gar is the Gar that people see, talk to, talk about. Private Gar is the unseen man, the man within, the conscience, the alter ego, the secret thoughts, the id.

11

Private Gar, the spirit, is invisible to everybody, always. Nobody except Public Gar hears him talk. But even Public Gar, although he talks to Private Gar occasionally, never sees him and never *looks at him. One cannot look at one's alter ego.*

MUSIC

Mendelssohn's Violin Concerto in E Minor, Op. 64
Ceildhe music
'All Round My Hat'—First Verse.
'She Moved through the Fair'—Second Verse.
'California, Here I Come!'
'Give the Woman in the Bed more Porter.'

Episode I

[*Kitchen in the home of County Councillor S. B. O'Donnell who owns a general shop. As the curtain rises Madge, the housekeeper, enters from the scullery with a tray in her hands and finishes setting the table. She is a woman in her sixties. She walks as if her feet were precious. She pauses on her way past the shop door.*]

MADGE Gar! Your tea!

PUBLIC [*off*] Right!
    [*She finishes setting the table and is about to go to the scullery door when Public Gar marches on stage. He is ecstatic with joy and excitement: tomorrow morning he leaves for Philadelphia.*]

GAR [*singing*] 'Philadelphia, here I come, right back where I started from . . .' [*Breaks off and catches Madge*] Come on, Madge! What about an old time waltz!

MADGE Agh, will you leave me alone.
    [*He holds on to her and forces her to do a few steps as he sings in waltz time.*]

PUBLIC 'Where bowers of flowers bloom in the spring'—

MADGE [*struggling*] Stop it! Stop it! You brat you!

PUBLIC Madge, you dance like an angel. [*Suddenly lets her go and springs away from her.*] Oh, but you'd give a fella bad thoughts very quick!

15

MADGE And the smell of fish of you, you dirty thing!
[*He grabs her again and puts his face up to hers, very confidentially.*]

PUBLIC Will you miss me?

MADGE Let me on with my work!

PUBLIC The truth!

MADGE Agh, will you quit it, will you?

PUBLIC I'll tickle you till you squeal for mercy.

MADGE Please, Gar ...

PUBLIC [*tickling her*] Will you miss me, I said?

MADGE I will—I will—I will—I——

PUBLIC That's better. Now tell me: What time is it?

MADGE Agh, Gar——

PUBLIC What time is it?

MADGE [*looking at clock*] Ten past seven.

PUBLIC And what time do I knock off at?

MADGE At seven.

PUBLIC Which means that on my last day with him he got ten minutes overtime out of my hide. [*He releases Madge.*] Instead of saying to me: [*grandly*] 'Gar, my son, since you are leaving me forever, you may have the entire day free,' what does he do? Lines up five packs of flour and says: [*in flat dreary tones*] 'Make them up into two-pound pokes.'

MADGE He's losing a treasure, indeed!

PUBLIC So d'you know what I said to him? I just drew myself up and looked him straight in the eye and said to him: 'Two-pound pokes it will be'— just like that.

MADGE That flattened him.
[*She goes off to the scullery. He stands at the door and talks in to her.*]

PUBLIC And that wasn't it all. At six o'clock he

16

remembered about the bloody pollock, and him in the middle of the Angelus [*stands in imitation of the Father: head bowed, hands on chest. In flat tones*—) 'Behold-the-handmaid-of-the-Lord-Gut-and-salt-them-fish.' So by God I lashed so much salt on those bloody fish that any poor bugger that eats them will die of thirst. But when the corpses are strewn all over Ballybeg, where will I be? In the little old U.S.A.! Yip-eeeeee! (*He swings away from the scullery door and does a few exuberant steps as he sings*—) 'Philadelphia, here I come, rightah backah where Ah started from—' [*He goes into his bedroom, flings himself down on his bed, rests his head on his hands, and looks at the ceiling. Sings alternate lines of 'Philadelphia'—first half—with Private* [*off*]].

PUBLIC   It's all over.

PRIVATE [*off, in echo-chamber voice*] And it's all about to begin. It's all over.

PUBLIC   And all about to begin.

PRIVATE [*Now on*) Just think, Gar.

PUBLIC   Think . . .

PRIVATE Think. . . . Up in that big bugger of a jet, with its snout pointing straight for the States, and its tail belching smoke over Ireland; and you sitting up at the front [*Public acts this*] with your competent fingers poised over the controls; and then away down below in the Atlantic you see a bloody bugger of an Irish boat out fishing for bloody pollock and——
         [*Public nose-dives, engines screaming, machine guns stuttering.*]

PUBLIC   Rat-tat-tat-tat-tat-tat-tat-tat-tat-tat.

PRIVATE Abandon ship! Make for the life-boats! Send for

Canon Mick O'Byrne!
[*Public gains altitude and nose-dives again.*]

PUBLIC Rat-tat-tat-tat-tat-tat-tat-tat-tat.

PRIVATE To hell with women and children! Say an Act of
Contrition!

PUBLIC Yip-eeeee!
[*He finishes taking off the shop coat, rolls it into a
bundle, and places it carefully on the floor.*]

PRIVATE It looks as if—I can't see very well from the
distance—but it looks as if—yes!—yes!—the free
is being taken by dashing Gar O'Donnell [*Public
gets back from the coat, poises himself to kick it*] pride
of the Ballybeg team. [*In commentator's hushed
voice*] O'Donnell is now moving back, taking a
slow, calculating look at the goal, I've never
seen this boy in the brilliant form he's in today—
absolute magic in his feet. He's now in position,
running up, and——
[*Public kicks the shop coat into the air.*]

PUBLIC Ya-hoooo! [*Sings and gyrates at same time.*)
'Philah-delph-yah, heah Ah come, rightah backah
weah Ah stahted from, boom-boom-boom-
boom——'
[*He breaks off suddenly when Private addresses him
in sombre tones of a judge.*]

PRIVATE Gareth Mary O'Donnell.
[*Public springs to attention, salutes, and holds this
absurd military stance. He is immediately inside his
bedroom door, facing it.*]

PUBLIC Sir.

PRIVATE You are full conscious of all the consequences of
your decision?

PUBLIC Yessir.

PRIVATE Of leaving the country of your birth, the land of

the curlew and the snipe, the Aran sweater and
the Irish Sweepstakes?

PUBLIC [*with fitting hesitation*] I-I-I-I have considered all
these, Sir.

PRIVATE Of going to a profane, irreligious, pagan
country of gross materialism?

PUBLIC I am fully sensitive to this, Sir.

PRIVATE Where the devil himself holds sway, and lust—
abhorrent lust—is everywhere indulged in
shamelessly?
[*Public winks extravagantly and nudges an imaginary
man beside him.*]

PUBLIC Who are you tellin'? [*Poker-stiff again.*]
Shamelessly, Sir, shamelessly.
[*Madge has entered from the scullery, carrying an old
suitcase and a bundle of clothes.*]

PRIVATE And yet you persist in exposing yourself to these
frightful dangers?

PUBLIC I would submit, Sir, that these stories are slightly
exaggerated, Sir. For every door that opens——
[*Madge opens the bedroom door.*]

MADGE Oh! You put the heart across me there! Get out
of my road, will you, and quit eejiting about!

PUBLIC Madge, you're an aul duck.

MADGE Aye, so. There's the case. And there's a piece of
rope for I see the clasp's all rusted. And there's
your shirts and your winter vests and your heavy
socks. And you'll need to air them shirts before
you—Don't put them smelly hands on them!

PUBLIC Sorry!

MADGE See that they're well aired before you put them
on. He's said nothing since, I suppose?

PUBLIC Not a word.

PRIVATE The bugger.

19

MADGE But he hasn't paid you your week's wages?

PUBLIC £3 15s—that'll carry me far.

MADGE He'll have something to say then, you'll see. And maybe he'll slip you a couple of extra pounds.

PUBLIC Whether he says good-bye to me or not, or whether he slips me a few miserable quid or not, it's a matter of total indifference to me, Madge.

MADGE Aye, so. Your tea's on the table—but that's a matter of total indifference to me.

PUBLIC Give me time to wash, will you?

MADGE And another thing: just because he doesn't say much doesn't mean that he hasn't feelings like the rest of us.

PUBLIC Say much? He's said nothing!

MADGE He said nothing either when your mother died. It must have been near daybreak when he got to sleep last night. I could hear his bed creaking.

PUBLIC Well to hell with him——

MADGE [*leaving*] Don't come into your tea smelling like a lobster-pot.

PUBLIC If he wants to speak to me he knows where to find me! But I'm damned if I'm going to speak to him first!

[*Madge goes off to the scullery.*]

[*Calling after her*] And you can tell him I said that if you like!

PRIVATE What the hell do you care about him. Screwballs! Skinflint! Skittery Face! You're free of him and his stinking bloody shop. And tomorrow morning, boy, when that little ole plane gets up into the skies, you'll stick your head out the window [*Public acts this*] and spit down on the lot of them!

[*S.B. appears at the shop door. He is in his late*

20

*sixties. Wears a hat, a good dark suit, collar and tie,
black apron. S. B. O'Donnell is a responsible,
respectable citizen.*]

s.b. Gar!

[*Public reacts instinctively. Private keeps calm.*]

PRIVATE Let the bugger call.

s.b. [*louder*] Gar!

[*Instinct is stronger than reason: Public rushes to his
door and opens it. But as soon as he opens it and
looks out at his father he assumes in speech and
gesture a surly, taciturn gruffness. He always
behaves in this way when he is in his father's
company.*]

PUBLIC Aye?

s.b. How many coils of barbed-wire came in on the
mail-van this evening?

PUBLIC Two. Or was it 3?

s.b. That's what I'm asking you. It was you that
carried them into the yard.

PUBLIC There were two—no, no, no, three—yes, three
—or maybe it was . . . was it two?

s.b. Agh!

[*S.B. retires to the shop. Public and Private come
back into the bedroom.*]

PRIVATE What sort of a stupid bugger are you? Think,
man! You went out and stood yarning to Joe
the Post; then you carried one coil into the yard
and came out with the sack of spuds for the
parochial; then you carried in the second coil . . .
and put it in the corner . . . and came out again to
the van . . . and. . . . [*Public skips into the air.*] Ah,
what the hell odds! That's his headache, old
Nicodemus! After tomorrow a bloody roll of
barbed-wire will be a mere bagatelle to you. [*In*

21

cowboy accent.] Yeah, man. You see tham thar
plains stretchin' 's far th'eye can see, man? Well,
tham thar plains belongs to Garry the Kid. An'
Garry the Kid he don't go in for none of your
fancy fencin'. No siree. [*His eye lights on the fresh
laundry Madge brought in.*] And what'll you wear
on the plane tomorrow, old rooster, eh?
[*Public picks up a clean shirt, holds it to his chest, and
surveys himself in the small mirror above his wash-
hand-basin.*]
Pretty smart, eh?

PUBLIC Pretty smart.

PRIVATE Pretty sharp?

PUBLIC Pretty sharp.

PRIVATE Pretty ou-la-la?

PUBLIC Mais oui.

PRIVATE And not a bad looker, if I may say so.

PUBLIC You may. You may.

PRIVATE [*in heavy U.S. accent*] I'm Patrick Palinakis,
president of the biggest chain of biggest hotels
in the world. We're glad to have you, Mr
O'Donnell.

PUBLIC [*Sweet, demure*] And I'm glad to be here, Sir.

PRIVATE Handsomely said, young man. I hope you'll be
happy with us and work hard and one day
maybe you'll be president of the biggest chain of
biggest hotels in the world.

PUBLIC That's my ambition, Sir.

PRIVATE You are twenty-five years of age, Mr
O'Donnell?

PUBLIC Correct.

PRIVATE And you spent one year at University College
Dublin?

PUBLIC Yes, Sir.

PRIVATE Would you care to tell me why you abandoned your academic career, Mr O'Donnell?

PUBLIC [*with disarming simplicity*] Well, just before I sat my First Arts exam, Sir, I did an old Irish turas, or pilgrimage, where I spent several nights in devout prayer, Sir.

PRIVATE St Patrick's Pilgrimage—on Lough——?

PUBLIC St Harold's Cross, Sir. And it was there that I came to realize that a life of scholarship was not for me. So I returned to my father's business.

PRIVATE Yeah. You mentioned that your father was a businessman. What's his line?

PUBLIC Well, Sir, he has—what you would call—his finger in many pies—retail mostly—general dry goods—assorted patent drugs—hardware—ah— ah—dehydrated fish—men's king-size hose— snuffs from the exotic East . . . of Donegal—a confection for gourmets, known as Peggy's Leg —weedkiller—[*Suddenly breaking off: in his normal accent: rolling on the bed*—] Yahooooooo! It is now sixteen or seventeen years since I saw the Queen of France, then the Dauphiness, at Versailles——

PRIVATE Let's git packin', boy. Let's git that li'l ole saddle bag opened and let's git packin'. But first let's have a li'l ole music on the li'l ole phonograph. Yeah man. You bet. Ah reckon. Yessir.
[*Public puts a record on the player: First Movement, Mendelssohn's violin concerto. Public is preening himself before his performance, and while he is flexing his fingers and adjusting his bow-tie, Private announces in the reverential tones of a radio announcer*]

23

The main item in tonight's concert is the first
movement of the violin concerto in E minor,
opus 64, by Jacob Ludwig Felix Mendelssohn.
The orchestra is conducted by Gareth O'Donnell
and the soloist is the Ballybeg half-back, Gareth
O'Donnell. Music critics throughout the world
claim that O'Donnell's simultaneous wielding of
baton and bow is the greatest thing since
Leather Ass died. Mendelssohn's Violin
Concerto, 3rd movement.
[*Private sits demurely on the chair. Public clears
his throat. Now Public plays the violin, conducts,
plays the violin, conducts, etc. etc. This keeps up for
some time. Then Private rises from his chair*]
Agh, come on, come on, come on! Less aul
foolin'. To work, old rooster, to work. [*Public
stops. Turns player down low and changes from the
first to the second movement Takes a look at the
case Madge brought in.*] Ah, hell, how can any
bloody bugger head into a jet plane with aul'
cardboard rubbish like that! [*Public examines the
surface.*] Damnit, maybe you could give it a lick
of paint! Or wash it! [*Public spits on the lid and
rubs it with his finger.*] God, you'll rub a hole in
the damn thing if you're not careful! Maybe aul
Screwballs'll slip you a fiver tonight and you
can get a new one in Dublin.

PUBLIC What a hope!
[*Public opens the case and sniffs the inside.*]
PRIVATE Oh! Stinks of cat's pee!
[*Public lifts out a sheet of faded newspaper.*]
PUBLIC [*reads*] The *Clarion*—1st January 1937.
PRIVATE Precious medieval manuscript . . . my God, was

it? . . . By God it was—the day they were married—and it [*the case*] hasn't been opened since their honeymoon . . . she and old Screwballs off on a side-car to Bundoran for three days. . . .

PUBLIC O God, the Creator and Redeemer of all the faithful, give to the soul of Maire, my mother, the remission of all her sins, that she may obtain. . . .

PRIVATE She was small, Madge says, and wild, and young, Madge says, from a place called Bailtefree beyond the mountains; and her eyes were bright, and her hair was loose, and she carried her shoes under her arm until she came to the edge of the village, Madge says, and then she put them on. . . .

PUBLIC Eternal rest grant unto her, O Lord, and let perpetual light shine. . . .

PRIVATE She was nineteen and he was forty, and he owned a shop, and he wore a soft hat, and she thought he was the grandest gentleman that ever lived, Madge says; and he—he couldn't take his eyes off her, Madge says. . . .

PUBLIC O God, O God the Creator and Redeemer. . . .

PRIVATE And sometimes in that first year, when she was pregnant with you, laddybuck, the other young girls from Bailtefree would call in here to dress up on their way to a dance, Madge says, and her face would light up too, Madge says. . . . [*Public puts the newspaper carefully inside the folds of a shirt.*] . . . And he must have known, old Screwballs, he must have known, Madge says, for many a night he must have heard her crying herself to sleep . . . and maybe it was good of

25

God to take her away three days after you were born. . . . [*Suddenly boisterous.*] Damn you, anyhow, for a bloody stupid bastard! It is now sixteen or seventeen years since I saw the Queen of France, then the Dauphiness, at Versailles! And to hell with that bloody mushy fidler! [*Public goes quickly to the record-player and sings boisterously as he goes.*]

PUBLIC 'Philadelphia, here I come——'

PRIVATE Watch yourself, nut-head. If you let yourself slip that way, you might find that——

PUBLIC '—right back where I started from.' [*Public has taken off the Mendelssohn and is now searching for another.*]

PRIVATE Something lively! Something bloody animal! A bit of aul thumpety-thump! [*Public puts on the record.*] An' you jist keep atalkin' to you'self all the time, Mistah, 'cos once you stop atalkin' to you'self ah reckon then you jist begin to think kinda crazy things—[*The record begins—Any lively piece of Ceilidhe Band music.*] Ahhhhh!

PUBLIC Yipeeeeeeeee! [*Public dances up and down the length of his bedroom. Occasionally he leaps high into the air or does a neat bit of foot-work. Occasionally he lilts. Occasionally he talks to different people he meets on the dance floor.*] Righ-too-del-loo-del-oo-del-oo-del-oo-del-oo-del-ah, Rum-ta-del-ah-del-ah-del-agh-del-ah-del-ah-del-agh. Hell of a crowd here the night, eh? Yah-ho! Man, you're looking powerful! Great! [*Private sits on the chair and watches. When he*

26

speaks his voice is soft. Public pretends not to hear him.]

PRIVATE Remember—that was Katie's tune. You
needn't pretend you have forgotten.
And it reminds you of the night the two of you
made all the plans, and you thought your heart
would burst with happiness.

PUBLIC [*louder*] Tigh-righ-tigh-righ-scal-del-de-da-del-
ah, Come on! A dirty big swing! Yaaaaaaaaaaah!

PRIVATE [*quietly, rapidly insisting*] Are you going to take
her photograph to the States with you? When
are you going to say good-bye to her? Will you
write to her? Will you send her cards and
photographs? You loved her once, old rooster;
you wanted so much to marry her that it was a
bloody sickness. Tell me, randy boy; tell me the
truth: have you got over that sickness? Do you
still love her? Do you still lust after her? Well,
do you? Do you? Do you?

PUBLIC Bugger!
[*Public suddenly stops dancing, switches—almost
knocks—off the record-player, pulls a wallet out of
his hip pocket and produces a snap. He sits and
looks at it.*]

PRIVATE Shhhhhhhhhhhhh. . . .

PUBLIC [*softly*] Kate . . . sweet Katie Doogan . . . my
darling Kathy Doogan. . . .

PRIVATE [*in same soft tone*] Aul bitch. [*Loudly.*] Rotten aul
snobby bitch! Just like her stinking rotten father
and mother—a bugger and a buggeress—a
buggeroo and a buggerette!

PUBLIC No, no; my fault—all my fault——

PRIVATE [*remembering and recalling tauntingly*] By God,
that was a night, boy, eh? By God, you made a

27

right bloody cow's ass of yourself. [*Public goes off right.*] Remember—when was it?—10 months ago?—you had just come back from a walk out the Mill Road, and the pair of you had the whole thing planned: engaged at Christmas, married at Easter, and 14 of a family—7 boys and 7 girls. Cripes, you make me laugh! You bloody-well make me die laughing. You were going to 'develop' the hardware lines and she was going to take charge of the 'drapery'! The drapery! The fishy socks and the shoebox of cotton spools and rusted needles! And you— you were to ask Screwballs for a rise in pay— 'in view of your increased responsibilities'! And you were so far gone that night, Laddybuck,— [*Public and Kate enter from the left and walk very slowly across the front of the stage. They stop and kiss. Then they move on again.*]—So bloody-well astray in the head with 'love' that you went and blabbed about your secret egg deals that nobody knew anything about—not even Madge! Stupid bloody get! O my God, how you stick yourself I'll never know!

PUBLIC   Kate—Kathy—I'm mad about you: I'll never last till Easter! I'll—I'll—I'll bloody-well burst! [*He catches her again and kisses her.*]

PRIVATE   Steady, boy, steady. You know what the Canon says: long passionate kisses in lonely places. . . .

PUBLIC   Our daughters'll all be gentle and frail and silly, like you; and our sons—they'll be thick bloody louts, sexy goats, like me, and by God I'll beat the tar out of them!

KATE   But £3 15s Gar! We could never live on that.

PUBLIC   [*kissing her hair*] Mmmm.

KATE   Gar! Listen! Be sensible.

PUBLIC Mmm?

KATE   How will we *live*?

PRIVATE [*imitating*] 'How will we *live*?'

PUBLIC Like lords—free house, free light, free fuel, free
        groceries! And every night at seven when we
        close—except Saturday; he stays open till damn
        near midnight on Saturdays, making out bloody
        bills; and sure God and the world knows that
        sending out bills here is as hopeless as peeing
        against the wind. .—

KATE   Gar! No matter what you say we just couldn't
        live on that much money. It—it's not possible.
        We'll need to have more security than that.

PUBLIC Maybe he'll die—tonight—of galloping
        consumption!

KATE   Gar. . . .

PUBLIC What's troubling you?
        [*He tries to kiss her again and she avoids him.*]

KATE   Please. This is serious.

PRIVATE 'Please. This is serious.'

PUBLIC [*irritably*] What is it?

KATE   You'll have to see about getting more money.

PUBLIC Of course I'll see about getting more money!
        Haven't I told you I'm going to ask for a rise?

KATE   But will he——?

PUBLIC I'll get it; don't you worry; I'll get it. Besides:
        [*with dignity*] I have a—a-a source of income that
        he knows nothing about—that nobody knows
        nothing about—knows anything about.

KATE   [*with joy*] Investments? Like Daddy?

PUBLIC Well . . . sort of . . . [*quickly*]. You know when
        I go round the country every Tuesday and
        Thursday in the lorry?

KATE Yes?

PUBLIC Well, I buy eggs direct from the farms and sell them privately to McLaughlin's Hotel—[winks] —for a handsome profit—[quickly]—but he knows nothing about it.

KATE And how much do you make?

PUBLIC It varies—depending on the time of year.

KATE Roughly.

PUBLIC Oh, anything from 12s 6d to £1.

KATE Every Tuesday and Thursday?

PUBLIC Every month. [Grabs her again.] God, Kate, I can't even wait till Christmas!

KATE Shhhhh.

PUBLIC But I can't. We'll have to get married sooner— next month—next week——

PRIVATE Steady, steady. . . .

PUBLIC Kate . . . my sweet Katie . . . my darling Kathy. . . .
[They kiss. Suddenly Kate breaks off. Her voice is urgent.]

KATE We'll go now, rightaway, and tell them.

PUBLIC Who?

KATE Mammy and Daddy. They're at home tonight.
[She catches his arm and pulls him towards the left.] Come on. Quickly. Now, Gar, now.

PUBLIC [adjusting his tie] God, Kathy, I'm in no—look at the shoes—the trousers——

KATE What matter. It must be now, Gar, now!

PUBLIC What—what—what'll I say?

KATE That you want their permission to marry me next week.

PUBLIC God, they'll wipe the bloody floor with me!

KATE Gar!
[She kisses him passionately, quickly, then breaks off

30

and goes. Stage right, now lit. A room in Doogan's house.]

PUBLIC God, my legs are trembling! Kathy. . . .

KATE Anybody at home? Mammy! Daddy!
[*Public hesitates before entering Doogan's house. Private is at his elbow, prompting him desperately.*]

PRIVATE Mr Doogan . . . —Senator Doogan—I want to ask your permission. . . . O my God! . . .

KATE Yo-ho!

PRIVATE Mrs Doogan, Kate and I have to get married rightaway—Cripes, no!——

KATE Where is everybody! Yo-ho-yo-ho!

PRIVATE If the boys could see you now!
[*Kate comes back to him, gives him a quick kiss on the cheek.*]

KATE Don't look so miserable. Here . . . [*fixes his tie*].

PUBLIC Kathy, maybe we should wait until—until—until next Sunday——

KATE [*earnestly*] Remember, it's up to you, entirely up to you.

DOOGAN [*off*] That you, Kate?

KATE [*rapidly*] You have £20 a week and £5,000 in the bank and your father's about to retire.
[*Turning and smiling at Doogan who has now entered.*] Just Gar and I, Daddy.
[*Doogan, Lawyer, Senator, middle forties.*]

DOOGAN Hello, Gareth. You're a stranger.

PRIVATE Speak, you dummy you!

KATE [*filling in*] Where's Mammy?

DOOGAN She's watching TV. [*To Gar.*] And how are things with you, Gareth?

PUBLIC Mr Doogan, I want——

PRIVATE Go on.

PUBLIC I won't be staying long.

31

DOOGAN [*to Kate*] Francis arrived when you were out. Took a few days off and decided to come north.

PRIVATE Cripes!

KATE He—he's—he's here—now?

DOOGAN Inside with your mother. Ask them to join us, will you?

[*Kate gives Public a last significant look.*]

KATE You talk to Daddy, Gar.

PRIVATE God, I will, I will.

[*Kate goes off right.*]

DOOGAN You've met Francis King, haven't you, Gareth?

PUBLIC Yes—yes——

PRIVATE King of the bloody fairies!

DOOGAN We don't want to raise Kate's hopes unduly, but strictly between ourselves there's a good chance that he'll get the new dispensary job here.

PUBLIC Kate's hopes?

DOOGAN Didn't she tell you? No, I can see she didn't. Of course there's nothing official yet; not even what you might call an understanding. But if this post does fall into his lap, well, her mother and I . . . let's say we're living in hope. A fine boy, Francis; and we've known the Kings, oh, since away back. As a matter of fact his father and I were class-fellows at school. . . .

[*Doogan goes on and on. We catch an occasional word. Meantime Private has moved up to Public's elbow.*]

PRIVATE Cripes, man!

DOOGAN . . . and then later at university when he did medicine and I did law, we knocked about quite a bit. . . .

32

PRIVATE O God, the aul bitch! Cripes, you look a right
fool standing there—the father of 14 children!—
Get out, you eejit you! Get out! Get out
quick before the others come in and die
laughing at you! And all the time she must
have known—the aul bitch!—And you
promised to give her breakfast in bed every
morning! And you told her about the egg
money!

DOOGAN . . . your father, Gareth?

PRIVATE He's talking to you, thick-skull.

PUBLIC What—what—what's that?

DOOGAN Your father—how is he?

PUBLIC Oh he—he—he's grand, thanks.

PRIVATE Get out! Get out!

PUBLIC Look Mr Doogan, if you'll excuse me, I think
I'd better move on——

DOOGAN Aren't you waiting for supper? The others will
be along in a moment for——

PUBLIC No, I must run. I've got to make up half-a-
hundredweight of sugar bags.

PRIVATE Brilliant!

PUBLIC Say good-bye to——

DOOGAN Certainly—certainly. Oh, Gareth—[*Public
pauses*].
[*Awkwardly, with sincerity.*] Kate is our only
child, Gareth, and her happiness is all that is
important to us——

PRIVATE [*sings*] 'Give the woman in the bed more
porter——'

DOOGAN What I'm trying to say is that any decision she
makes will be her own—

PRIVATE '—Give the man beside her water, Give the
woman in the bed more porter,——'

33

DOOGAN   Just in case you should think that her mother
            or I were . . . in case you might have the
            idea. . . .

PUBLIC   [*rapidly*] Good night, Mr Doogan.
            [*Public rushes off.*]

DOOGAN   Good-bye. . . . Gareth.
            [*Doogan stands lighting his pipe.*]

KATE   [*Enters down right of Doogan and sees that Gar
            is no longer there*] Where's Gar?

DOOGAN   He didn't seem anxious to stay.

KATE   But didn't he—did he——?

DOOGAN   No, he didn't. [*He crosses Kate to exit down right
            as light fades to black out.*]
            [*Black out Doogan's room. Public and Private move
            back to the bedroom where Public is putting away
            the photograph and begins washing.*]

PRIVATE [*wearily*] Mrs Doctor Francis King. September
            8th. In harvest sunshine. Red carpet and white
            lilies and Sean Horgan singing 'Bless This
            House'—and him whipped off to Sligo jail two
            days later for stealing turf. Honeymoon in
            Mallorca and you couldn't have afforded to take
            her to Malahide. By God, Gar, aul sod, it was a
            sore hoke on the aul prestige, eh? Between
            ourselves, aul son, in the privacy of the
            bedroom, between you and me and the wall, as
            the fella says, has it left a deep scar on the aul
            skitter of a soul, eh? What I mean to say like,
            you took it sort of bad, between you and me
            and the wall, as the fella says——

PUBLIC   [*sings*] 'Philadelphia, here I come, right back——"

PRIVATE But then there's more fish in the sea, as the fella
            says, and they're all the same when they're

34

upside down; and between you and me and the wall, the first thing you would have had to do would have been to give the boot to Daddy Senator. And I'm thinking, Gar, aul rooster, that wouldn't have made you his pet son-in-law. Mister Fair-play Lawyer Senator Doogan—'her happiness is all that is important to us'! You know, of course, that he carries one of those wee black cards in the inside pocket of his jacket, privately printed for him: 'I am a Catholic. In case of accident send for a bishop.' And you know, too, that in his spare time he travels for maternity corsets; and that he's a double spy for the Knights and the Masons; and that he takes pornographic photographs of Mrs D. and sends them anonymously to reverend mothers. And when you think of a bugger like that, you want to get down on your knees and thank God for aul Screwballs. [*Imitating his father's slow speech.*] So you're going to America in the morning, son?

[*Public carries on with his washing and dressing and at the same time does this dialogue.*]

PUBLIC   Yes, Father.

PRIVATE   Nothing like it to broaden the mind. Man, how I'd love to travel. But there's some it doesn't agree with—like me, there.

PUBLIC   In what way, Father?

PRIVATE   The bowels, son. Let me move an inch from the house here—and they stall.

PUBLIC   No!

PRIVATE   Like the time I went to Lough Derg, away back in '35. Not a budge. The bare feet were nothing to the agonies I went through. I was bound up for two full weeks afterwards.

PUBLIC It taught you a lesson.

PRIVATE Didn't it just? Now I wouldn't even think of travelling.

PUBLIC Anchored by the ass.

PRIVATE Bound by the bowels.

PUBLIC Tethered by the toilet. Tragic.
[*Public has now finished dressing. He surveys himself in the mirror.*]

PRIVATE Not bad. Not bad at all. And well preserved for a father of 14 children.

PUBLIC [*in absurd Hollywood style*] Hi, gorgeous! You live in my block?

PRIVATE [*matching the accent*] Yeah, big handsome boy. Sure do.

PUBLIC Mind if I walk you past the incinerator, to the elevator?

PRIVATE You're welcome, slick operator.
[*Public is facing the door of his bedroom. Madge enters the kitchen from the scullery.*]

PUBLIC What'ya say, li'l chick, you and me—you know —I'll spell it out for ya ifya like. [*Winks, and clicks his tongue.*]

PRIVATE You say the cutest things, big handsome boy!

PUBLIC A malted milk at the corner drug-store?

PRIVATE Wow!

PUBLIC A movie at the downtown drive-in?

PRIVATE Wow-wow!

PUBLIC Two hamburgers, two cokes, two slices of blueberry pie?

PRIVATE Wow-wow-wow.

PUBLIC And then in my apartment——
[*Madge enters the bedroom.*]

36

MADGE Gee, Mary, and Jay! Will you quit them antics!

PUBLIC Well, you should knock anyway before you enter a man's room!

MADGE Man! I bathed you every Saturday night till you were a big lout of fourteen! Your tea's cold waiting. [*She makes towards door.*]
[*She goes into the kitchen. Public and Private follow her.*]

PUBLIC How was I to know that?

MADGE Amn't I hoarse calling you? Dear, but you're in for a cooling when you go across! [*As she passes through the shop door on way to scullery.*] Boss!

PRIVATE [*in imitation*] 'Boss!'
[*She pauses at the scullery door. With shy delight.*]

MADGE I forgot to tell you. Nelly had a wee baby this morning.

PUBLIC Go on!

MADGE A wee girl. 7 lb 4 oz.

PUBLIC How many's that you have now?

MADGE Four grandnieces and three grandnephews. [*Pause.*] And they're going to call this one Madge—at least so she *says*.

PUBLIC I'll send it a—a—a—an elephant out of my first wages! An elephant for wee Madge!

MADGE I had a feeling it would be a wee girl this time. Maybe I'll take a run over on Sunday and square the place up for her. She could do with some help, with seven of them.

PUBLIC You're a brick, Madge.

MADGE Aye, so. [*As she goes to scullery.*] Wee Madge, maybe. . . .
[*Public sits at the table. Private leans against the wall beside him.*]

PRIVATE And now what are you sad about? Just because

37

she lives for those Mulhern children, and gives
them whatever few half-pence she has? Madge,
Madge, I think I love you more than any of
them. Give me a piece of your courage, Madge.
[*S.B. enters from the shop and goes through his
nightly routine. He hangs up the shop keys. He looks
at his pocket watch and checks its time with the clock
on the wall. He takes off his apron, folds it carefully,
and leaves it on the back of his chair. Then he sits
down to eat. During all these ponderous jobs Private
keeps up the following chatter:*]
And here comes your pleasure, your little ray of
sunshine. Ladies and Gentlemen, I give you—
the one and only—the inimitable—the
irrepressible—the irresistible—County
Councillor—S—B—O'Donnell! [*Trumpet—
hummed—fanfare. Continues in the smooth, unctuous
tones of the commentator at a mannequin parade.*]
And this time Marie Celeste is wearing a cheeky
little head-dress by Pamela of Park Avenue,
eminently suitable for cocktail parties, morning
coffee, or just casual shopping. It is of brown
Viennese felt, and contrasts boldly with the
attractive beach ensemble, created by Simon.
The pert little apron is detachable—[*S.B. removes
apron*]—thank you, Marie Celeste—and under-
neath we have the tapered Italian-line slacks in
ocelot. I would draw your attention to the large
collar stud which is highly decorative and can be
purchased separately at our boutique. We call
this seductive outfit 'Indiscretion'. It can be worn
six days a week, in or out of bed. [*In polite tone.*]
Have a seat Screwballs. [*S.B. sits down at the
table.*] Thank you. Remove the hat. [*S.B. takes*

off the hat to say grace. He blesses himself.] On
again. [*Hat on.*] Perfectly trained; the most
obedient father I ever had. And now for our
nightly lesson in the English language. Repeat
slowly after me: Another day over.

S.B. Another day over.

PRIVATE Good. Next phrase. I suppose we can't complain.

S.B. I suppose we can't complain.

PRIVATE Not bad. Now for a little free conversation. But
no obscenities, Father dear; the child is only
twenty-five. [*S.B. eats in silence. Pause.*] Well,
come on, come on! Where's that old rapier wit
of yours, the toast of the Ballybeg coffee houses?

S.B. Did you set the rat-trap in the store?

PUBLIC Aye.

PRIVATE [*hysterically*] Isn't he a riot! Oh my God, that
father of yours just kills me! But wait—wait—
shhh-shhh——

S.B. I didn't find as many about the year.

PRIVATE Oooooh God! Priceless! Beautiful! Delightful!
'I didn't find as many about the year!' Did you
ever hear the beat of that? Wonderful! But
isn't he in form tonight? But isn't he? You
know, it's not every night that jewels like that,
pearls of wisdom on rodent reproduction, drop
from those lips! But hold it—hold it——!
[*S.B. takes out a handkerchief, removes his teeth,
wraps them in the handkerchief, and puts them in
his pocket.*]
[*Private exhales with satisfaction.*]

PRIVATE Ah! That's what we were waiting for; complete
informality; total relaxation between intimates.
Now we can carry on. Screwballs. [*Pause.*] I'm
addressing you, Screwballs.

[*S.B. clears his throat.*]

Thank you. [*As the following speech goes on all trace of humour fades from Private's voice. He becomes more and more intense and it is with an effort that he keeps his voice under control.*] Screwballs, we've eaten together like this for the past twenty-odd years, and never once in all that time have you made as much as one unpredictable remark. Now, even though you refuse to acknowledge the fact, Screwballs, I'm leaving you forever. I'm going to Philadelphia, to work in an hotel. And you know why I'm going, Screwballs, don't you. Because I'm twenty-five, and you treat me as if I were five—I can't order even a dozen loaves without getting your permission. Because you pay me less than you pay Madge. But worse, far worse than that, Screwballs, because—*we embarrass one another.* If one of us were to say, 'You're looking tired' or 'That's a bad cough you have', the other would fall over backways with embarrassment. So tonight d'you know what I want you to do? I want you to make one unpredictable remark, and even though I'll still be on that plane tomorrow morning, I'll have doubts: Maybe I should have stuck it out; maybe the old codger did have feelings; maybe I have maligned the old bastard. So now, Screwballs, say . . . [*thinks*] . . . 'Once upon a time a rainbow ended in our garden' . . . say, 'I like to walk across the White Strand when there's a misty rain falling' . . . say, 'Gar, son—' say, 'Gar, you bugger you, why don't you stick it out here with me for it's not such a bad aul bugger of a place.' Go on. Say it!

40

Say it! Say it!

S.B. True enough. . . .

PUBLIC [*almost inaudibly*] Aye?

S.B. I didn't find as many about the year.

PUBLIC [*roars*] Madge! Madge!

S.B. No need to roar like that.

PUBLIC The—the—the—bread's done. We need more bread.

S.B. You know where it's kept, don't you?
[*Madge at scullery door.*]

PUBLIC Can we have more bread, Madge . . . please. . . .

MADGE Huh! Pity you lost the power of your legs.

PUBLIC I'll—I'll get it myself—it doesn't matter. . . .
[*Madge comes over to the table and takes the plate from Public. She gives S.B. a hard look.*]

MADGE [*irony*] The chatting in this place would deafen a body. Won't the house be quiet soon enough —long enough?
[*She shuffles off with the plate.*]

PRIVATE Tick-tock-tick-tock-tick-tock. It is now sixteen or seventeen years since I saw the Queen of France, then the Dauphiness, at Versailles. . . . Go on! What's the next line?
[*S.B. produces a roll of money from his pocket and puts it on the table.*]

S.B. I suppose you'll be looking for your pay.

PUBLIC I earned it.

S.B. I'm not saying you didn't. It's all there—you needn't count it.

PUBLIC I didn't say I was going to count it, did I?

PRIVATE Tick-tock-tick-tock-tick-tock——

PUBLIC More tea?

S.B. Sure you know I never take a second cup.

PRIVATE [*imitating*] 'Sure you know I never take a second

41

cup.' [*Brittle and bright again.*] Okay, okay, okay,
it's better this way, Screwballs, isn't it? You
can't teach new tricks to two old dogs like us.
In the meantime there's a little matter I'd like to
discuss with you, Screwballs . . . [*with
exaggerated embarrassment*] it's—it's nothing really
. . . it's just something I'm rather hesitant to
bring up, but I'm advised by the very best
Church authorities that you'll be only too glad
to discuss it with your son. Admittedly we're
both a bit late in attacking the issue now, but—
ha—you see——
[*Madge enters with a plate of bread. Private makes a
very obvious show of changing the subject.*]
Oh marvellous weather—truly wonderful for the
time of year—a real heat wave—all things
considered——

MADGE   A body couldn't get a word in edgeways with
you two!

PRIVATE   Madge has such a keen sense of humour, don't
you agree? I love people with a sense of humour,
don't you? It's the first thing I look for in a
person. I seize them by the throat and say to
them, 'Have you a sense of humour?' And then,
if they have, I feel—I feel *at home* with them
immediately. . . . But where was I? Oh, yes—
our little talk—I'm beginning to wonder,
Screwballs—I suspect—I'm afraid—[*in a rush,
ashamed*]—I think I'm a sex-maniac! [*Throws his
hands up.*] Please, please don't cry, Screwballs;
please don't say anything; and above all please
don't stop eating. Just—just let me talk a bit
more—let me communicate with someone—
that's what they all advise—communicate—pour

42

out your pent-up feelings into a sympathetic ear. So all I ask for the moment is that you listen— just listen to me. As I said, I suspect that that I'm an s.-m. [*Rapidly, in self-defence.*] But I'm not the only one, Screwballs; oh indeed I am not; and all the boys around—some of them are far worse than I am. [*As if he had been asked the question.*] Why? Why do I think we're all s.-m.s? Well, because none of us is married. Because we're never done boasting about the number of hot courts we know—and the point is we're all virgins. Because——

[*Voices off.*]

Shhhh! Someone's coming. Not a word to anybody. This is our secret. Scouts' honour.

[*Enter Master Boyle from the scullery. He is around sixty, white-haired, handsome, defiant. He is shabbily dressed; his eyes, head, hands, arms are constantly moving—he sits for a moment and rises again—he puts his hands in his pocket and takes them out again—his eyes roam around the room but see nothing. S.B. is barely courteous to him.*]

S.B. Oh, good night, Master Boyle. How are you doing?

PUBLIC Master.

BOYLE Sean. Gar. No, no, don't stir. I only dropped in for a second.

PUBLIC Sit over and join us.

BOYLE No. I'm not stopping.

S.B. Here's a seat for you. I was about to go out to the shop anyway to square up a bit.

BOYLE Don't let me hold you back.

S.B. I'll be in again before you leave, Master.

BOYLE If you have work to do. . . .

43

PRIVATE [*to S.B.*] Ignorant bastard! [*Looking at Boyle.*] On his way to the pub! God, but he's a sorry wreck too, arrogant and pathetic. And yet whatever it is about you. . . .

BOYLE Tomorrow morning, isn't it?

PUBLIC Quarter past seven. I'm getting the mail van the length of Strabane.

BOYLE You're doing the right thing, of course. You'll never regret it. I gather it's a vast restless place that doesn't give a curse about the past; and that's the way things should be. Impermanence and anonymity—it offers great attractions. You've heard about the latest to-do?

PUBLIC Another row with the Canon? I really hadn't heard——

BOYLE But the point is he can't sack me! The organization's behind me and he can't budge me. Still, it's a . . . a bitter victory to hold on to a job when your manager wants rid of you.

PUBLIC Sure everybody knows the kind of the Canon, Master.

BOYLE I didn't tell you, did I, that I may be going out there myself?

PRIVATE Poor bastard.

BOYLE I've been offered a big post in Boston, head of education in a reputable university there. They've given me three months to think it over. What are you going to do?

PUBLIC Work in an hotel.

BOYLE You have a job waiting for you?

PUBLIC In Philadelphia.

BOYLE You'll do all right. You're young and strong and of average intelligence.

PRIVATE Good old Boyle. Get the dig in.

BOYLE Yes, it was as ugly and as squalid as all the other
to-dos—before the whole school—the priest and
the teacher—dedicated moulders of the mind.
You're going to stay with friends?

PUBLIC With Aunt Lizzy.

BOYLE Of course.

PRIVATE Go on. Try him.

PUBLIC You knew her, didn't you, Master?

BOYLE Yes, I knew all the Gallagher girls: Lizzy, Una,
Rose, Agnes. . . .

PRIVATE And Maire, my mother, did you love her?

BOYLE A long, long time ago . . . in the past. . . . He
comes in to see your father every night, doesn't
he?

PUBLIC The Canon? Oh, it's usually much later than
this——

BOYLE I think so much about him that—ha—I feel a
peculiar attachment for him. Funny, isn't it?
Do you remember the Christmas you sent me
the packet of cigarettes? And the day you
brought me a pot of jam to the digs? It was you,
wasn't it?

PRIVATE Poor Boyle——

BOYLE All children are born with generosity. Three
months they gave me to make up my mind.

PUBLIC I remember very well——

BOYLE By the way—[*producing a small book*] a—little
something to remind you of your old teacher—
my poems——

PUBLIC Thank you very much.

BOYLE I had them printed privately last month. Some
of them are a bit mawkish but you'll not notice
any distinction.

PUBLIC I'm very grateful, Master.

45

BOYLE I'm not going to give you advice, Gar. Is that clock right? Not that you would heed it even if I did; you were always obstinate——

PRIVATE Tch, tch.

BOYLE But I would suggest that you strike out on your own as soon as you find your feet out there. Don't keep looking back over your shoulder. Be 100 per cent American.

PUBLIC I'll do that.

BOYLE There's an inscription on the fly-leaf. By the way, Gar, you couldn't lend me 10s until—ha—I was going to say until next week but you'll be gone by then.

PUBLIC Surely, surely.

BOYLE I seem to have come out without my wallet. . . .

PRIVATE Give him the quid.

[*Public gives over a note. Boyle does not look at it.*]

BOYLE Fine. I'll move on now. Yes, I knew all the Gallagher girls from Bailtefree, long, long ago. Maire and Una and Rose and Lizzy and Agnes and Maire, your mother. . . .

PRIVATE You might have been my father.

BOYLE Oh, another thing I meant to ask you: should you come across any newspapers or magazines over there that might be interested in an occasional poem, perhaps you would send me some addresses——

PUBLIC I'll keep an eye out.

BOYLE Not that I write as much as I should. You know how you get caught up in things. But you have your packing to do, and I'm talking too much as usual.

[*He holds out his hand and they shake hands. He does not release Public's hand.*]

46

Good luck, Gareth.

PUBLIC Thanks, Master.

BOYLE Forget Ballybeg and Ireland.

PUBLIC It's easier said.

BOYLE Perhaps you'll write me.

PUBLIC I will indeed.

BOYLE Yes, the first year. Maybe the second. I'll—I'll miss you, Gar.

PRIVATE For God's sake get a grip on yourself.

PUBLIC Thanks for the book and for——
[*Boyle embraces Public briefly.*]

PRIVATE Stop it! Stop it! Stop it!
[*Boyle breaks away and goes quickly off through the scullery. He bumps into Madge who is entering.*]

MADGE Lord, the speed of him! His tongue out for a drink!

PRIVATE Quick! Into your room!

MADGE God knows I don't blame the Canon for wanting rid of that——
[*Public rushes to the bedroom. Private follows.*]
Well! The manners about this place!
[*She gathers up the tea things. Public stands inside the bedroom door, his hands up to his face. Private stands at his elbow, speaking urgently into his ear.*]

PRIVATE Remember—you're going! At 7.15. You're still going! He's nothing but a drunken aul schoolmaster—a conceited, arrogant wash-out!

PUBLIC O God, the Creator and Redeemer of all the faithful——

PRIVATE Get a grip on yourself! Don't be a damned sentimental fool! [*Sings.*] 'Philadelphia, here I come——'

PUBLIC Maire and Una and Rose and Agnes and Lizzy

and Maire——

PRIVATE Yessir, you're going to cut a bit of a dash in them thar States! Great big sexy dames and night clubs and high living and films and dances and——

PUBLIC Kathy, my own darling Kathy——

PRIVATE [*sings*] 'Where bowers of flowers bloom in the spring'

PUBLIC I don't—I can't.

PRIVATE [*sings*] 'Each morning at dawning, everything is bright and gay/A sun-kissed miss says Don't be late—' Sing up, man!

PUBLIC I—I—I——

PRIVATE [*sings*] 'That's why I can hardly wait.'

PUBLIC [*sings limply*] 'Philadelphia, here I come.'

PRIVATE That's it, laddybuck!

TOGETHER
'Philadelphia, here I come.'

Curtain

END OF EPISODE I: FIRST INTERVAL

Episode II

[*A short time later. Public is lying on the bed, his hands behind his head. Private is slumped in the chair, almost as if he were dozing. Public sings absently.*]

PUBLIC [*sings*]

> Last night she came to me, she came softly in,
> So softly she came that her feet made no din,
> And laid her hand on me, and this she did say,
> 'It will not be long love till our wedding day'.

[*When the singing stops there is a moment of silence. Then, suddenly, Private springs to his feet.*]

PRIVATE What the bloody hell are you at, O'Donnell? Snap out of it, man! Get up and keep active! The devil makes work for idle hands! It is now sixteen or seventeen years since I saw the Queen of France, then the Dauphiness, at Versailles. [*Public goes off the bed and begins taking clothes from the chest of drawers and putting them into his case.*]

PRIVATE [*lilting to a mad air of his own making*] Ta-ra-del-oo-del-ah-dol-de-dol-de-dol-del-ah—[*continuing as rapidly as he can speak*]—Tell me this and tell me no more: Why does a hen cross the road?

PUBLIC Why?

PRIVATE To get to the other side. Ha-ha! Why does a hen lay an egg?

PUBLIC Why?

PRIVATE Because it can't lay a brick. Yo-ho. Why does a sailor wear a round hat?

PUBLIC Why?

PRIVATE To cover his head. Hee-hee-hee. Nought out of three; very bad for a man of average intelligence. That's the style. Keep working; keep the mind active and well stretched by knowing the best that is thought and written in the world, and you wouldn't call Daddy Senator your father-in-law. [*Sings.*]

> *Give the woman in the bed more porter*
> *Give the man beside her water*
> *Give the woman in the bed more porter*
> *More porter for the woman in the bed.*

[*Confidentially.*] D'you know what I think laddie; I mean, just looking at you there.

PUBLIC What?

PRIVATE You'd make a hell of a fine President of the United States.

[*Public straightens up and for a second surveys the room with the keen eye of a politician. Relaxes again.*]

PUBLIC Agh!

PRIVATE But you would!

PUBLIC You need to be born an American citizen.

PRIVATE True for you. What about Chairman of General Motors?

[*Public shrugs indifferently.*]

Boss of the Teamsters' Union?

[*Public shrugs his indifference.*]

PRIVATE Hollywood—what about Hollywood?

PUBLIC   Not what it was.

PRIVATE   Damnit but you're hard to please too. Still,
there must be something great in store for you.
[*Cracks his fingers at his brainwave.*] The U.S.
Senate! Senator Gareth O'Donnell, Chairman of
the Foreign Aid Committee!
[*He interviews Public who continues packing his
clothes busily.*]
Is there something you would like to say,
Senator, before you publish the findings of your
committee?

PUBLIC   Nothing to say.

PRIVATE   Just a few words.

PUBLIC   No comment.

PRIVATE   Isn't it a fact that suspicion has fallen on Senator
Doogan?

PUBLIC   Nothing further to add.

PRIVATE   Did your investigators not discover that Senator
Doogan is the grandfather of fourteen unborn
illegitimate children? That he sold his daughter
to the king of the fairies for a crock of gold?
That a Chinese spy known to the FBI as
Screwballs——

PUBLIC   Screwballs?

PRIVATE   Screwballs.

PUBLIC   Describe him.

PRIVATE   Tall, blond, athletic-looking——

PUBLIC   Military moustache?

PRIVATE   —very handsome; uses a diamond-studded
cigarette-holder.

PUBLIC   Usually accompanied by a dark seductive woman
in a low-cut evening gown?

PRIVATE   —wears a monocle, fluent command of
languages——

PUBLIC But seldom speaks? A man of few words?

PRIVATE —drives a cream convertible, villas in Istanbul, Cairo and Budapest——

PUBLIC [*Declaims*] Merchant Prince, licensed to deal in tobacco——

PRIVATE An' sowl! That's me man! To a T! The point is—what'll we do with him?

PUBLIC Sell him to a harem?

PRIVATE Hide his cascara sagrada?
[*Madge comes into the kitchen to lift the tablecloth.*]

PUBLIC [*serious*] Shhh!

PRIVATE The boys? Is it the boys? To say good-bye?

PUBLIC Shhhh!

PRIVATE It's Madge—aul fluke-feet Madge.
[*They both stand listening to the sound of Madge flapping across the kitchen and out to the scullery.*]

PUBLIC [*calls softly*] Madge.
[*Private drops into the armchair. Public stands listening until the sound has died away.*]

PRIVATE [*wearily*] Off again! You know what you're doing, don't you, laddybuck? Collecting memories and images and impressions that are going to make you bloody miserable; and in a way that's what you want, isn't it?

PUBLIC Bugger!
[*Private springs to his feet again. With forced animation.*]

PRIVATE Bugger's right! Bugger's absolutely correct! Back to the job! Keep occupied. Be methodical.
　　Eanie-meanie-minie-mow
　　Catch-the-baby-by-the-toe.
Will all passengers holding immigration visas please come this way.
[*Public produces documents from a drawer. He checks*

54

them.]

PRIVATE Passport?

PUBLIC Passport.

PRIVATE Visa?

PUBLIC Visa.

PRIVATE Vaccination cert.?

PUBLIC Vaccination cert.

PRIVATE Currency?

PUBLIC Eighty dollars

PRIVATE Sponsorship papers?

PUBLIC Signed by Mr Conal Sweeney.

PRIVATE Uncle Con and Aunt Lizzy. Who made the whole thing possible. Read her letter again— strictly for belly-laughs.

PUBLIC [*reads*] Dear Nephew Gar, Just a line to let you know that your Uncle Con and me have finalized all the plans——

PRIVATE Uncle Con and I.

PUBLIC —and we will meet you at the airport and welcome you and bring you to our apartment which you will see is located in a pretty nice locality and you will have the spare room which has TV and air-conditioning and window meshes and your own bathroom with a shower——

PRIVATE Adjacent to RC church. No children. Other help kept.

PUBLIC You will begin at the Emperor Hotel on Monday 23rd which is only about twenty minutes away.

PRIVATE Monsieur, madam.

PUBLIC Con says it is a fine place for to work in and the owner is Mr Patrick Palinakis who is half-Irish——

55

PRIVATE Patrick.

PUBLIC —and half-Greek.

PRIVATE Palinakis.

PUBLIC His grandfather came from County Mayo.

PRIVATE By the hokey! The Greek from Belmullet!

PUBLIC We know you will like it here and work hard.

PRIVATE [*rapidly*] Monsieur-madam-monsieur-madam-
monsieur-madam——

PUBLIC We remember our short trip to Ireland last
September with happy thoughts and look forward to seeing you again. Sorry we missed
your father that day. We had Ben Burton in to
dinner last evening. He sends his regards.

PRIVATE Right sort, Ben.

PUBLIC Until we see you at the airport, all love, Elise.

PRIVATE 'Elise'! Damnit, Lizzy Gallagher, but you came
on in the world.

PUBLIC P.S. About paying back the passage money
which you mentioned in your last letter—
desist!—no one's crying about it.

PRIVATE Aye, Ben Burton was a right skin.

PUBLIC [*remembering*] September 8th.

PRIVATE By God Lizzy was in right talking form that
day——

PUBLIC 'You are invited to attend the wedding of Miss
Kathleen Doogan of Gortmore House——'

PRIVATE [*snaps*] Shut up, O'Donnell! You've got to quit
this moody drivelling! [*Coaxing.*] They arrived
in the afternoon; remember? A beautiful quiet
harvest day, the sun shining, not a breath of
wind; and you were on your best behaviour.
And Madge—remember? Madge was as huffy as
hell with the carry-on of them, and you couldn't
take your eyes off Aunt Lizzy, your mother's

56

sister—so this was your mother's sister—
remember?

[*Three people have moved into the kitchen: Con
Sweeney, Lizzy Sweeney, and Ben Burton. All
three are in the fifty-five to sixty region. Burton is
American, the Sweeneys Irish-American. Con
Sweeney sits at the kitchen table with Ben Burton.
Lizzy moves around in the centre of the kitchen.
Public stands at the door of his bedroom. Private
hovers around close to Public. The three guests have
glasses in their hands. None of them is drunk, but
Lizzy is more than usually garrulous. She is a small
energetic woman, heavily made-up, impulsive. Con,
her husband, is a quiet, patient man. Burton, their
friend, sits smiling at his glass most of the time.
As she talks Lizzy moves from one to the other, and
she has the habit of putting her arm around, or catching
the elbow of, the person she is addressing. This
constant physical touching is new and disquieting to
Public. A long laugh from Lizzy:*]

LIZZY Anyhow, there we are, all sitting like stuffed
ducks in the front seat—Una and Agnes and
Rose and Mother and me—you know—and
mother dickied up in her good black shawl and
everything—and up at the altar rails there's
Maire all by herself and her shoulders are sorta
working—you know—and you couldn't tell
whether she was crying or giggling—she was a
helluva one for giggling—but maybe she was
crying that morning—I don't know——

CON Get on with the story, honey.

LIZZY [*with dignity*] Would you please desist from
bustin' in on me?

[*Con spreads his hands in resignation.*]

57

LIZZY But listen to this—this'll kill you—Mother's here, see? And Agnes is here and I'm here. And Agnes leans across Mother to me—you know—and she says in this helluva loud voice—she says —[*laughs*]—this really does kill me—she says— in this whisper of hers—and you know the size of Bailtefree chapel; couldn't swing a cat in that place—[*suddenly anxious.*] That chapel's still there, isn't it? It hasn't fell down or nothing, has it?

CON [*dryly*] Unless it fell down within the last couple of hours. We drove up there this morning. Remember?

LIZZY [*relieved*] Yeah. So we did. Fine place. Made me feel kinda—you know—what the hell was I talking about?

BEN Agnes leaned over to you and said——
[*Lizzy puts her arm around him and kisses the crown of his head.*]

LIZZY Thanks, Ben. A great friend with a great memory! I'll tell you, Gar, Ben Burton's one hundred per cent. The first and best friend we made when we went out. [*To Con.*] Right, honey?

CON Right.

LIZZY Way back in '37.

CON '38.

LIZZY [*loudly*] October 23rd, 19 and 37 we sailed for the United States of America. [*Con spreads his hands.*] Nothing in our pockets. No job to go to. And what does Ben do?

CON A guy in a million.

LIZZY He gives us this apartment. He gives us dough. He gives us three meals a day—until bonzo

58

LIZZY [*Con*] finally gets himself this job. Looks after us like we were his own skin and bone. Right, honey?

CON Right.

LIZZY So don't let nobody say nothing against Ben Burton. Then when he [*Con*] gets this job in this downtown store——

CON First job was with the construction company.

LIZZY Would you please desist? [*Con spreads hands.*] His first job was with Young and Pecks, hauling out them packing cases and things; and then he moved to the construction company, and *then* we got a place of our own.

PUBLIC You were telling us about that morning.

LIZZY What's he talking about?

PUBLIC The day my father and mother got married.

LIZZY That day! Wasn't that something? With the wind howling and the rain slashing about! And Mother, poor Mother, may God be good to her, she thought that just because Maire got this guy with a big store we should all of got guys with big stores. And poor Maire—we were so alike in every way, Maire and me. But he was good to her. I'll say that for S.B. O'Donnell—real good to her. Where the hell is he anyhow? Why will S. B. O'Donnell, my brother-in-law, not meet me?

CON He [*Public*], told you—he's away at a wedding.

LIZZY What wedding?

CON Some local girl and some Dublin doc.

LIZZY What local girl? You think I'm a stranger here or something?

CON [*to Public*] What local girl?

PUBLIC Senator Doogan's daughter.

PRIVATE Kathy.

59

LIZZY Never heard of him. Some Johnny-hop-up.
When did they start having Senators about this
place for Gawds sakes?

BEN [to Public] You have a senate in Dublin, just like
our Senate, don't you?

LIZZY Don't you start telling me nothing about my
own country, Ben. You got your own problems
to look after. Just you leave me to manage this
place, okay?

BEN Sorry, Elise.

LIZZY Ben! [She kisses the top of his head.] Only that
I'm a good Irish-American Catholic—[to Public]
and believe me, they don't come much better
than that—and only that I'm stuck with
Rudolph Valentino [Con], I'd take a chance
with Ben Burton any day [kisses him again]
black Lutheran and all that he is.
[Madge appears at the door of the shop. She refuses
to look at the visitors. Her face is tight with
disapproval. Her accent is very precise.]

MADGE Are there any *Clarions* to spare or are they all
ordered?

PUBLIC They're all ordered, Madge.

LIZZY Doing big deals out there, honey, huh?

MADGE Thank you, Gareth.
[Madge withdraws.]

LIZZY 'Thank you, Gareth!' [She giggles to herself].

CON Honey! [To Public.] You'll think about what we
were discussing?

PUBLIC I will, Uncle Con.

CON The job's as good as you'll get and we'd be
proud to have you.

LIZZY Don't force him.

CON I'm not forcing him. I'm only telling him.

60

LIZZY   Well now, you've told him—a dozen times. So
        now desist, will you?
        [Con spreads his hands.]
PUBLIC I will think about it. Really.
LIZZY   Sure! Sure! Typical Irish! He will think about
        it! And while he's thinking about it the store
        falls in about his head! What age are you?
        Twenty-four? Twenty-five? What are you
        waiting for? For S.B. to run away to sea? Until
        the weather gets better?
CON   Honey!
LIZZY   I'm talking straight to the kid! He's Maire's boy
        and I've got an interest in him—the only
        nephew I have. [To Ben.] Am I right or am I
        wrong?
BEN   I'm still up in Bailtefree chapel.
LIZZY   Where? [Confidentially to Con.] Give him no
        more to drink. [Patiently to Ben.] You're sitting in
        the home of S. B. O'Donnell and my deceased
        sister, Maire, Ben.
CON   You were telling us a story about the morning
        they got married, honey, in Bailtefree chapel.
LIZZY   Yeah, I know, I know, but you keep busting in
        on me.
PUBLIC You were about to tell us what Agnes whispered
        to you.
LIZZY   [crying] Poor Aggie—dead. Maire—dead. Rose,
        Una, Lizzy—dead—all gone—all dead and gone.
        . . .
CON   Honey, you're Lizzy.
LIZZY   So what?
CON   Honey, you're not dead.
LIZZY   [regarding Con cautiously] You gone senile all of a
        sudden? [Confidentially to Ben.] Give him no

61

more to drink. [*To Con.*] For Gawds sakes who
says I'm dead?

BEN You're very much alive, Elise.
[*She goes to him and gives him another kiss.*]

LIZZY Thank you, Ben. A great friend with a great
intellect. Only one thing wrong with Ben
Burton: he's a black Baptist.

BEN Just for the record, Gar, I'm Episcopalian.

LIZZY Episcopalian—Lutheran—Baptist—what's the
difference? As our pastor, Father O'Flaherty,
says—'My dear brethren,' he says, 'Let the
whole cart-load of them, and the whole zoo of
them, be to thee as the Pharisee and the
publican.'

CON Honey!

LIZZY But he's still the best friend we have. And we
have many good, dear, kind friends in the US:
Right, honey?

CON Right.

LIZZY But when it comes to holding a candle to Ben
Burton—look—comparisons are—he's not in the
halfpenny place with them!

BEN [*laughing*] Bang on, Elise!

LIZZY Am I right or am I wrong?

CON Honey!

LIZZY [*to Public*] And that's why I say to you:
America's Gawd's own country. Ben?

BEN Don't ask me. I was born there.

LIZZY What d'ya mean—'Don't ask me'? I am asking
you. He should come out or he should not—
which is it?

BEN It's just another place to live, Elise. Ireland—
America—what's the difference?

LIZZY You tell him, honey. You tell him the set-up

62

Jim True (left) with Robert Sean Leonard as Gar Public and Private.

\notos of the 1994 Roundabout Theatre Company production by Carol Rosegg.

Public and Private Gar with Madge (Pauline Flanagan at center) and S.B. (Milo O'Shea at left).

lic and Private Gar with Kate Doogan (Miriam Healey-Louie at center).

Public and Private Gar with Master Boyle (Jarlath Conroy at right).

we have. [*Now with growing urgency, to Public.*]
We have this ground-floor apartment, see, and a
car that's air-conditioned, and colour TV, and
this big collection of all the Irish records you
ever heard, and 15,000 bucks in Federal Bonds—

CON Honey.

LIZZY —and a deep freezer and—and—and a back
yard with this great big cherry tree, and squirrels
and night-owls and the smell of lavender in the
spring and long summer evenings and snow at
Christmas and a Christmas tree in the parlour
and—and—and——

CON Elise. . . .

LIZZY And it's all so Gawd-awful because we have no
one to share it with us. . . . [*She begins to sob.*]

CON [*softly*] It's okay, honey, okay. . . .

LIZZY He's my sister's boy—the only child of five
girls of us——

BEN I'll get the car round the front.
[*Ben goes off through the scullery.*]

LIZZY —and we spent a fortune on doctors, didn't we,
Connie, but it was no good, and then I says to
him [*Con*], 'We'll go home to Ireland', I says,
'and Maire's boy, we'll offer him everything we
have——'

PRIVATE [*terrified*] No. No.

LIZZY '—everything, and maybe we could coax him—
you know——' maybe it was sorta bribery—I
dunno—but he would have everything we ever
gathered——

PRIVATE Keep it! Keep it!

LIZZY —and all the love we had in us——

PRIVATE No! No!

CON Honey, we've a long drive back to the hotel.

63

LIZZY [*trying to control herself*] That was always the kind
of us Gallagher girls, wasn't it . . . either
laughing or crying . . . you know, sorta silly and
impetuous, shooting our big mouths off, talking
too much, not like the O'Donnells—you know—
kinda cold——

PRIVATE Don't man, don't.

CON Your gloves, honey. It's been a heavy day.

LIZZY [*to Public, with uncertain dignity*] Tell your father
that we regret we did not have the opportunity
for to make his acquaintance again after all
these——

PUBLIC [*impetuously*] I want to go to America—if you'll
have me——

PRIVATE Laddy!

CON Sure. You think about it, son. You think about it.

PUBLIC Now—as soon as I can, Aunt Lizzy—I mean it—

LIZZY Gar? [*To Con, as if for confirmation.*] Honey?

CON Look son——

LIZZY To us, Gar? To come to us? To our home?

CON Ben's waiting, Elise.

PUBLIC If you'll have me. . . .

LIZZY If we'll have him, he says; he says if we'll have
him! That's why I'm here! That's why I'm
half-shot-up!
[*She opens her arms and approaches him.*]
Oh Gar, my son——

PRIVATE Not yet! Don't touch me yet!
[*Lizzy throws her arms around him and cries
happily.*]

LIZZY My son, Gar, Gar, Gar. . . .

PRIVATE [*softly, with happy anguish*] God . . . my God . . .
Oh my God. . . .

(BLACK OUT)

64

PRIVATE [*When the bedroom light goes up Public and Private are there. The kitchen is empty. Public bangs the lid of his case shut and Private stands beside him, jeering at him. While this taunting goes on Public tries to escape by fussing about the room.*]

PRIVATE September 8th, the sun shining, not a breath of wind—and this was your mother's sister— remember. And that's how you were got! Right, honey? Silly and impetuous like a Gallagher! Regrets?

PUBLIC None.

PRIVATE Uncertainties?

PUBLIC None.

PRIVATE Little tiny niggling reservations?

PUBLIC None.

PRIVATE Her grammar?

PUBLIC Shut up!

PRIVATE But, honey, wasn't it something?

PUBLIC Go to hell.

PRIVATE Her vulgarity?

PUBLIC Bugger off.

PRIVATE She'll tuck you into your air-conditioned cot every night.
[*Public, so that he won't hear, begins to whistle 'Philadelphia, Here I Come.'*]

PRIVATE And croon, 'Sleep well, my li'l honey child.'
[*Public whistles determinedly.*]
She got you soft on account of the day it was, didn't she?
[*Public whistles louder.*]
And because she said you were an O'Donnell— 'cold like'.

PUBLIC It is now sixteen or seventeen years since I saw the Queen of France——

65

PRIVATE But of course when she threw her arms around you—well, well, well!

PUBLIC —then the Dauphiness, at Versailles——

PRIVATE Poor little orphan boy!

PUBLIC Shut up! Shut up!

PRIVATE [*in child's voice*] Ma-ma. . . . Maa-ma.
[*Public flings open the bedroom door and dashes into the kitchen. Private follows behind.*]

PUBLIC Madge!

PRIVATE [*quietly, deliberately*] You don't want to go, laddybuck. Admit it. You don't want to go.
[*Madge enters from the scullery.*]

PUBLIC [*searching for an excuse*] I can't find my coat. I left it in my room.
[*Madge gives him a long, patient look, goes to the the nail below the school clock, lifts down the coat, and hands it to him. He takes it from her and goes towards the scullery door.*]

PUBLIC If you would only learn to leave things where you find them you wouldn't be such a bad aul nuisance.
[*Public and Private go off*].

MADGE [*calls*] Don't you dare come home drunk!
[*Public's head appears round the door.*]

PUBLIC [*softly*] I'm going to say good-bye to the boys over a quiet drink or two. And how I spend my nights is a matter entirely for myself.

MADGE 'The Boys!' Couldn't even come here to say good-bye to you on your last night.

PRIVATE Straight to the bone!

PUBLIC Just you mind your business and I'll mind mine.

MADGE How many of them are getting the pension now?

PUBLIC And in case you're in bed when I get back I

want a call at half-six.

MADGE The clock'll be set. If you hear it well and good.
[*Public disappears. Madge fusses about the kitchen
until S.B. enters from the shop. He has a newspaper
in his hand and sits at the top of the table. She
watches him as he reads. She adjusts a few things.
She looks back at him, then suddenly, on the point of
tears, she accuses him.*]

MADGE You sit there, night after night, year after year,
reading that aul paper, and not a tooth in your
head! If you had any decency in you at all, you
would keep them plates in while there's a lady
in your presence!

S.B. [*puzzled*] Eh?

MADGE I mean it. It—it—it—it just drives me mad, the
sight of you! [*The tears begin to come.*] And I
have that much work to do: the stairs have to
be washed down, and the store's to be swept,
and your room has to be done out—and—and—
I'm telling you I'll be that busy for the next
couple of weeks that I won't have time to lift
my head!
[*She dashes off. S.B. stares after her, then out at the
audience. Then, very slowly, he looks down at the
paper again—it has been upside down—and turns it
right side up. But he can't read. He looks across at
Gar's bedroom, sighs, rises, and exits very slowly to
the shop. Silence for a second after S.B. leaves.
The silence is suddenly shattered by the boisterous
arrival of the boys and Gar. We hear their
exaggerated laughter and talk outside before they
burst in. When they enter they take over the
kitchen, sprawling on chairs, hunting for tumblers for
the stout they produce from their pockets, taking long,*

*deep pulls on their cigarettes, giving the impression
that they are busy, purposeful, randy gents about to
embark on some exciting adventure. But their bluster
is not altogether convincing. There is something false
about it. Tranquility is their enemy: they fight it
valiantly. At the beginning of this scene Gar is
flattered that the boys have come to him. When they
consistently refuse to acknowledge his leaving—or
perhaps because he is already spiritually gone from
them—his good humour deserts him. He becomes
apart from the others. Ned is the leader of the group.
Tom is his feed-man, subserviently watching for
every cue. Joe, the youngest of the trio, and not yet
fully committed to the boys' way of life, is torn
between fealty to Ned and Tom and a spontaneous
and simple loneliness over Gar's departure. Nothing
would suit him better than a grand loud send-off
party. But he cannot manage this, and his loyalty is
divided. He is patently gauche, innocent, obvious.*

NED There's only one way to put the fear of God up
them bastards—[*points to his boot*]—every time—
you know where.

JOE Who's the ref, Ned?

TOM Jimmy Pat Barney from Bunmornan. [*Guardedly
to Public.*] Where's the aul fella?

PUBLIC Haven't a bloody clue. Probably in the shop.
Relax, man.

NED That [*the boot*] or the knee—it's the only game
them gets can play; and we can play it too.

TOM [*relaxing*] They've a hell of a forward line all the
same, Ned.

NED They'll be in crutches this day week. By God, I
can hardly wait to get the studs planted in wee
Bagser Doran's face! [*He crashes his fist into the*

68

palm of his hand.]

TOM All the same, Jimmy Pat Barney's the get would put you off very quick.

NED He won't say a word to me. He knows his match when he meets it.
[*Tom laughs appreciatively. Madge appears at the scullery door.*]

MADGE [*coldly*] Just thought I heard somebody whispering. So youse finally made it.

JOE [*holding up glass*] True to our word, Madge, that's us!

PUBLIC [*happily*] They were on their way here when I ran into them.

MADGE Aye, so. [*Ned belches.*] Mister Sweeney, too; gentlemanly as ever.

NED [*slapping his knee*] Come on away over here and I'll take some of the starch out of you, Madge Mulhern. How long is since a fella gripped your knee? Haaaaaaaaaaa!

MADGE None of your smutty talk here, Mister Sweeney. And if the boss comes in and finds them bottles——

PUBLIC I'll keep them in order, Madge.

MADGE 'Boys'! How are you!
[*She goes out.*]

TOM [*calling*] You're jealous because you're past it— that's what's wrong with you. Right, Ned?

PUBLIC [*raising glass*] Well, boys, when you're lining out on the pitch, you can think of me, because I'll be thinking of you.

JOE [*earnestly*] Lucky bloody man, Gar. God, I wish I was in your——

NED [*quickly*] By the way, lads, who's the blondie thing I seen at the last Mass on Sunday?

69

TOM A big red-head?

NED Are you bloody-well deaf! A blondie! She wouldn't be Maggie Hanna's niece, would she?

TOM There was two of them, sitting over near the box?

NED I seen one.

TOM 'Cos they're English. Staying at the hotel. But the big red thing—she's one of Neil McFadden's girls.

NED Annie? Is Annie home?

JOE Aye, she is. So I heard the mammy saying.

NED Bloody great! That's me fixed up for the next two weeks! Were any of youse ever on that job?

JOE No, I wasn't, Ned.

TOM For God's sake, she wouldn't spit on you!

NED Game as they're going, big Annie. But you need the constitution of a horse. I had her for the fortnight she was home last year and she damned near killed me.

PUBLIC Big Annie from up beyond the quarry?

JOE You know, Gar—the one with the squint.

NED [with dignity] Annie McFadden has no squint.

PUBLIC Away and take a running race to yourself, Ned.

NED [with quiet threat] What do you mean?

PUBLIC You were never out with big Annie McFadden in your puff, man.

NED Are you calling me a liar?

PRIVATE [wearily] What's the point.

TOM [quickly] Oh, by God, Ned was there, Gar, manys and manys the time. Weren't you, Ned?

PUBLIC Have it your own way.

JOE [nervously] And maybe she got the squint straightened out since I saw her last. All the

70

women get the squints straightened out nowadays. Damnit, you could walk from here to
Cork nowadays and you wouldn't see a woman
with a——

NED I just don't like fellas getting snottery with me,
that's all.
[*There follows an uneasy silence during which
Private surveys the group.*]

PRIVATE The boys. . . . They weren't always like this,
were they? There was a hell of a lot of crack,
wasn't there? There was a hell of a lot of
laughing, wasn't there?

TOM [*briskly*] Bit of life about the place next week,
lads—the Carnival. Too bad you'll miss it, Gar.
By God it was a holy fright last year, night
after night. [*To Ned.*] Remember?

NED [*sulkily*] Bloody cows, the whole bloody lot of
them!

TOM Mind the night with the two wee Greenock
pieces?

NED [*thawing*] Aw, stop, stop!

TOM Talk about hot things!

NED Liveliest wee tramps I ever laid!

TOM And the fat one from Dublin you picked up at
the dance that night—the one that hauled you
down into the ditch!

NED I was never the same since.

TOM [*to Public*] Whatever it is about him [*Ned*], if
there's a fast woman in the country, she'll go for
Ned first thing. Lucky bugger! [*Pause.*] Aye,
lucky bugger!
[*Another brief silence. These silences occur like
regular cadences. To defeat them someone always
introduces a fresh theme.*]

PUBLIC I'm for off tomorrow, boys.

NED [*indifferently*] Aye, so, so. . . .

TOM Brooklyn, isn't it?

PUBLIC Philadelphia.

TOM Philadelphia. That's where Jimmy Crerand went to, isn't it? Philadelphia. . . .

NED [*quickly*] Mind the night Jimmy and us went down to the caves with them Dublin skivvies that was working up at the Lodge? [*To Public.*] Were you?—No, you weren't with us that night.

JOE Was I there, Ned?

NED You mind the size of Jimmy?—five foot nothing and scared of his shadow.

PUBLIC Best goalie we ever had.

NED One of the women was Gladys and the other was Emmy or something——

TOM Damnit, I mind now! Gladys and Emmy—that was it, Ned!

NED Anyhow the rest of us went in for a swim——

TOM In the bloody pelt!

NED —and your man Jimmy was left in the cave with the women; and what the hell do they do but whip the trousers off him!

JOE No, I wasn't there that night.

NED And the next thing we see is wee Jimmy coming shouting across the White Strand and the two Dublin cows haring after him.

TOM Not a stab on him!

NED —and him squealing at the top of his voice, 'Save me, boys, save me!'

TOM Never drew breath till he reached home!

NED You [*Gar*] missed that night.

TOM 'Save me, boys, save me!'

NED I don't think we went to bed that night at all.

72

TOM You may be sure we didn't.

NED Powerful.

[*Another silence descends. After a few seconds Private speaks*]:

PRIVATE We were all there that night, Ned. And the girls' names were Gladys and Susan. And they sat on the rocks dangling their feet in the water. And we sat in the cave, peeping out at them. And then Jimmy Crerand suggested that we go in for a swim; and we all ran to the far end of the shore; and we splashed about like schoolboys. Then we came back to the cave, and wrestled with one another. And then out of sheer boredom, Tom, you suggested that we take the trousers off Crerand—just to prove how manly we all were. But when Ned started towards Jimmy—five foot nothing, remember?—wee Jimmy squared up and defied not only the brave Ned but the whole lot of us. So we straggled back home, one behind the other, and left the girls dangling their feet in the water. And that was that night.

PUBLIC If the ground's not too hard, you'll do well on Sunday.

NED Hard or soft—[*examining his boot*]—I've a couple of aul scores to settle.

PUBLIC You'll never get as good a half-back as the one you're losing.

NED [*quickly, with pretended interest*] D'you know what I'm thinking? We'd better see about transport.

TOM Damnit, you're right. I'll get the aul fella's van easy enough. Can you get your Charlie's lorry?

NED Just maybe. I'd better try him the night.

JOE What about a song from Gar, boys, before we

break up?

NED What time is it?

JOE It's early in the night yet.

TOM Twenty past nine.

NED We'd better move then; Charlie was talking about going to a dance in Ardmore.

TOM Damnit, that's an idea!

JOE We'll all go—a big last night for Gar!

NED Ardmore? Are you mad? Bloody women in that place don't know what they're for!

TOM True for you. Scream their heads off if you laid a hand on them.

NED But I'll tell you what we'll do—call in home first to see Charlie and then go on to the hotel for a dirty big booze-up.

JOE I don't like drinking in that place.

NED Them two English bits—what's their name?

TOM Them strangers? Agh you wouldn't have a chance there. They do nothing but walk and look at weeds and stuff——

NED Who wouldn't have a chance?

TOM I know, Ned. But them two—they're sort of stiff-looking—like—like they worked in a post-office or something.

NED They're women, aren't they?

TOM Damnit, we might! . . . Still I don't know. . . . They knit a lot. . . . [*To Public.*] What d'you think?

JOE I vote we stay here.

PUBLIC And you can count me out. I've an early start.

NED £10 to a shilling I click with one or other of them!

PUBLIC I won't be here to collect my winnings.

NED Come on! Any takers? Never clapped eyes on

74

them and I'm offering ten notes to a bob!

TOM Cripes, I know that look in his eyes!

NED Wise bloody men! The blood's up, lads! Off to the front! Any volunteers for a big booze-up and a couple of women?

TOM Did he say women? Sign me on!

JOE I don't think I'm in form the night, boys——

NED We'll show them a weed or two, eh?

TOM Out to the sand-banks! Get them in the bloody bent!

NED We're away—Wait! Wait!—How much money have you?
[*They both produce their money—a fistful of small coins.*]

TOM 2s 6d . . . 2s 11d . . . 3s 3d . . . 3s 5½d.

NED And I have 6s 2d. It'll have to do. Say a prayer they're fast and thrifty.

TOM Dirty aul brute! Lead the way, Bull!

NED I'm telling you—the blood's up!

TOM Coming, lads?

PUBLIC I'm getting up at half six.

NED [*casually from the door*] So long, Gar. You know the aul rule—If you can't be good. . . .

TOM Send us a pack of them playing cards—the ones with the dirty pictures on the back!

NED And if the women are as easy as the money out there, we might think of joining you. [*To Tom.*] Right, old cock?

TOM Bull on regardless! Yaaaaaaaaaaah!
[*They open the door. Ned hesitates and begins taking off the broad leather belt with the huge brass buckle that supports his trousers.*]

NED [*shyly, awkwardly*] By the way, Gar, since I'll not see you again before you go——

TOM Hi! What are you at? At least wait till you're
     sure of the women!

NED [*impatiently to Tom*] Agh, shut up! [*To Public.*] If
     any of them Yankee scuts try to beat you up
     some dark night, you can . . . [*now he is very
     confused and flings the belt across the room to
     Public*] . . . you know . . . there's a bloody big
     buckle on it . . . manys a get I scutched with
     it. . . .

TOM Safe enough, lads: he has braces on as well!

NED I meant to buy you something good, but the aul
     fella didn't sell the calf to the jobbers last
     Friday . . . and he could have, the stupid
     bastard, such a bloody stupid bastard of an aul
     fella!

PUBLIC [*moved*] Thanks, Ned . . . thanks. . . .

JOE Damnit, I have nothing for you, Gar.

TOM [*quickly*] Are we for the sandbanks or are we
     not?

NED You'll make out all right over there . . . have
     a. . . .

TOM I know that look in his eyes!
     [*Ned wheels rapidly on Tom, gives him a more than
     playful punch, and says savagely.*]

NED Christ, if there's one get I hate, it's you!
     [*He goes off quickly.*]
     [*Tome looks uncertainly after him, looks back at
     Public, and says with dying conviction*]:

TOM The blood's up. . . . Oh by God, when he goes
     on like that, the . . . the blood's up all
     right. . . .
     [*Tom looks after Ned, then back to Joe and Gar, as
     if he can't decide which to join, then impetuously he
     dashes off after Ned, calling:*]

Hi! Ned, Ned, wait for me. . . .
[*There is a silence. Public is looking at the belt. Joe begins to fidget. Now Public becomes aware of him.*]

PUBLIC What the hell are you waiting for?

JOE Damnit, man, like it's your last night and all, and I thought——

PUBLIC Get to hell and run after them.

JOE Sure you know yourself they'll hang about the gable of the hotel and chat and do nothing.

PUBLIC For God's sake, man, those English women will be swept off their feet!

JOE [*uncertainly*] You're taking a hand at me now.

PUBLIC I'm telling you, you're missing the chance of a lifetime.

JOE Maybe—eh?—what d'you think?

PUBLIC Go on! Go on!

JOE God, maybe you're right. You never know what'll happen, eh? You finish that [*drink*] for me! God, maybe we'll click the night! Say a wee prayer we do! Cripes, my blood's up too! Where's my cap?
[*He graps the cap, dashes to the door, remembers he won't see Gar again.*]

JOE Send us a card, Gar, sometimes, eh?

PUBLIC Surely, Joe.

JOE Lucky bloody man. I wish I was you.

PUBLIC There's nothing stopping you, is there?

JOE Only that the mammy planted sycamore trees last year, and she says I can't go till they're tall enough to shelter the house.

PUBLIC You're stuck for another couple of days, then. Away off with you, man.

JOE Good luck, Gar. And tell Madge that the next time she asks us up for tea we'd bloody well better get it.

PUBLIC She *asked* you?

JOE That's why I was joking her about us keeping
our word. As if we wanted tea, for God's sake!
But I'd better catch up with the stirk before they
do damage. . . So long, aul cock!

[*He runs off.*]

PUBLIC Madge. . . . Oh God. . . .

[*Private moves over beside him. He speaks quickly,
savagely at first, spitting out the first three lines.
Gradually he softens, until the speech ends almost in
a whisper:*]

PRIVATE They're louts, ignorant bloody louts, and you've
always known it! And don't pretend you're
surprised; because you're not. And you know
what they'll do tonight, don't you? They'll
shuffle around the gable of the hotel and take an
odd furtive peep into the lounge at those
English women who won't even look up from
their frigid knitting! Many a time you did it
yourself, bucko! Aye, and but for Aunt Lizzy
and the grace of God, you'd be there tonight,
too, watching the lights go out over the village,
and hearing the front doors being bolted, and
seeing the blinds being raised; and you stamping
your feet to keep the numbness from spreading,
not wanting to go home, not yet for another
while, wanting to hold on to the night although
nothing can happen now, nothing at all. . . .
Joe and Tom and big, thick, generous Ned. . . .
No one will ever know or understand the fun
there was; for there *was* fun and there *was*
laughing—foolish, silly fun and foolish, silly
laughing; but what it was all about you can't

remember, can you? Just the memory of it—
that's all you have now—just the memory; and
even now, even so soon, it is being distilled of
all its coarseness; and what's left is going to be
precious, precious gold. . . .
[*There is a knock at the door. Public goes off to
answer it.*]

KATE [*off*] Hello, Gar.

PRIVATE Kate!

KATE [*on*] This isn't a healthy sign, drinking by
yourself.

PRIVATE Talk! Talk!

PUBLIC What—what are you doing here?

KATE I hear you're off to America.

PUBLIC First thing in the morning.

KATE You wouldn't think of calling to say good-bye
to your friends, I suppose?

PUBLIC I was going to, but I——

PRIVATE Careful!

PUBLIC —it went clean out of my mind. You know how
it is, getting ready. . . .

KATE I understand, Gar.

PRIVATE She's a married woman, you bugger!

KATE Philadelphia?

PUBLIC Yes. Take a seat.

KATE To an aunt, isn't it?

PUBLIC That's right. A sister of mother's.

KATE And you're going to work in a hotel.

PUBLIC You know as much about it as I do.

KATE You know Baile Beag—Small Town.

PUBLIC I'll probably go to night-school as well—you
know, at night——

PRIVATE Brilliant.

PUBLIC —do law or medicine or something——

79

PRIVATE Like hell! First Arts stumped you!

KATE You'll do well, Gar; make a lot of money, and come back here in twenty years' time, and buy the whole village.

PUBLIC Very likely. That's my plan anyhow.

PRIVATE Kate . . . Kathy. . . .

PUBLIC How's your father and mother?

KATE Fine, thanks. And Mr O'Donnell?

PUBLIC Grand, grand. Is Dr King well?

KATE I hear no complaints.

PRIVATE Then the Dauphiness of Versailles. And surely never lighted on this orb, which she hardly seemed to touch, a more delightful vision. I saw her just above the horizon, decorating and cheering the elevated sphere she just began to move in——

PUBLIC [*A shade louder than necessary*] I'll come home when I make my first million, driving a Cadillac and smoking cigars and taking movie-films.

KATE I hope you're very happy there and that life will be good to you.

PUBLIC [*slightly louder*] I'll make sure life's good to me from now on.

KATE Your father'll miss you.

PUBLIC [*rapidly, aggressively*] That's his look out! D'you know something? If I had to spend another week in Ballybeg, I'd go off my bloody head! This place would drive anybody crazy! Look around you, for God's sake! Look at Master Boyle! Look at my father! Look at the Canon! Look at the boys! Asylum cases, the whole bloody lot of them!

PRIVATE [*pained*] Shhhhhhh!

80

PUBLIC Listen, if someone were to come along to me
tonight and say, 'Ballybeg's yours—lock, stock,
and barrel,' it wouldn't make that [*cracks his
fingers*] much difference to me. If you're not
happy and content in a place—then—then—then
you're not happy and content in a place! It's as
simple as that. I've stuck around this hole far too
long. I'm telling you: it's a bloody quagmire, a
backwater, a dead-end! And everybody in it
goes crazy sooner or later! Everybody!

PRIVATE Shhhhhhhh. . . .

PUBLIC There's nothing about Ballybeg that I don't
know already. I hate the place, and every stone,
and every rock, and every piece of heather
around it! Hate it! Hate it! And the sooner that
plane whips me away, the better I'll like it!

KATE It isn't as bad as that, Gar.

PUBLIC You're stuck here! What else can you say!

PRIVATE That'll do!

PUBLIC And you'll die here! But I'm not stuck! I'm
free! Free as the bloody wind!

KATE All I meant was——

PUBLIC Answerable to nobody! All this bloody yap
about father and son and all this sentimental
rubbish about 'homeland' and 'birthplace'—yap!
Bloody yap! Impermanence—anonymity—that's
what I'm looking for; a vast restless place that
doesn't give a damn about the past. To hell
with Ballybeg, that's what I say!

PRIVATE Oh, man. . . .

KATE I'd better go. Francis'll be wondering what's
keeping me.

PUBLIC [*recklessly*] Tell him I was asking for him.

KATE Good-bye, Gar.

81

PUBLIC [*in same tone*] Enjoy yourself, Kate. And if you can't be good—you know?
[*Public goes off with Kate.*]
[*Off.*] Be sure to call the first one after me.
[*She is gone. Public returns and immediately buries his face in his hands.*]

PRIVATE Kate ... sweet Katie Doogan ... my darling Kathy Doogan. ...
[*Public uncovers his face and with trembling fingers lights a cigarette and takes a drink. As he does:*]

PRIVATE [*very softly*] Oh my God, steady man, steady—it is now sixteen or seventeen years since I saw the Queen of France, then the Dauphiness, at Versailles, and surely never lighted on this orb— Oh God, Oh my God, those thoughts are sinful— [*sings*] as beautiful Kitty one morning was tripping with a pitcher of milk——
Public attempts to whistle his song 'Philadelphia, Here I come.' He whistles the first phrase and the notes die away. Private keeps on talking while Public attempts to whistle.

PRIVATE We'll go now, right away, and tell them— Mammy and Daddy—they're at home tonight— now, Gar, now—it must be now—remember, it's up to you entirely up to you—gut and salt them fish—and they're going to call this one Madge, at least so she *says*——
[*Public makes another attempt to whistle.*]
—a little something to remind you of your old teacher—don't keep looking back over your shoulder, be 100 per cent American—a packet of cigarettes and a pot of jam—seven boys and seven girls—and our daughters'll be all gentle and frail and silly like you— and I'll never wait till

Christmas—I'll burst, I'll bloody-well burst—
good-bye, Gar, it isn't as bad as that—good-bye,
Gar, it isn't as bad as that—good-bye, Gar, it
isn't as bad as that——
PUBLIC [*in whispered shout*] Screwballs, say something!
Say something, father!

Quick Curtain

END OF EPISODE TWO: SECOND INTERVAL

Episode III

PART ONE

[A short time later. The rosary is being said. Public is kneeling with his back to the audience. S.B. is kneeling facing the audience. Madge is facing the shop door. Private kneels beside Public. Madge is saying her decade, and the other three—S.B. Public and Private—are answering. The words are barely distinct, a monotonous, somnolent drone. After a few moments Private lowers his body until his rear is resting on the backs of his legs. We cannot see Public's face. While Private talks, the rosary goes on.]

PRIVATE *[relaxing, yawning]* Ah-ho-ho-ho-ho-ho. This
time tomorrow night, bucko, you'll be saying
the rosary all by yourself—unless Lizzy and Con
say it *[ioins in a response in American accent]*—
Holy Mairy, Mother of Gawd, pray for us
sinners now and at the hour . . . *[he tails off as
his mind wanders again]*. No, not this time
tomorrow. It's only about half-four in Philadelphia now, and when it's half-nine there it'll
be the wee hours of the morning here; and
Screwballs'll be curled up and fast asleep in his
wee cot—*[To S.B.]*—right, honey? And when
he's dreaming, you'll be swaggering down 56th
Street on Third at the junction of 29th and
Seventh at 81st with this big blonde nuzzling

up to you—[*suddenly kneels erect again and responds in unison with Public. Keeps this up for two or three responses and slowly subsides again*]. You'd need to be careful out there, boy; some of those Yankee women are dynamite. But you'll never marry; never; bachelor's written all over you. Fated to be alone, a man without intimates; something of an enigma. Who is he, this silent one? Where is he from? Where does he go? Every night we see him walking beneath the trees along the bank of the canal, his black cloak swinging behind him, his eyes lost in thought, his servant following him at a respectful distance. [*In reply.*] Who is he? I'll tell you who he is: The Bachelor. All the same, laddybuck, there are compensations in being a bachelor. You'll age slowly and graciously, and then, perhaps, when you're quite old—about forty-three— you'll meet this beautiful girl of nineteen, and you'll fall madly in love. Karin—that's her name —no—ah—ah—Tamara—[*caressing the word*]. Tamara—grand-daughter of an exiled Russian prince, and you'll be consumed by a magnificent passion; and this night you'll invite her to dinner in your penthouse, and you'll be dressed in a deep blue velvet jacket, and the candles will discover magic fairy lights in her hair, and you'll say to her, 'Tamara,' and she'll incline her face towards you, and close her eyes, and whisper——

[*From a few seconds back the droning prayers have stopped. Now Madge leans over to Public and gives him a rough punch.*]

MADGE Your decade!

[*Private and Public jump erect again and in perfect unison give out their decade. Gradually, as the prayers continue, they relax into their slumped position.*]

PRIVATE When you're curled up in your wee cot, Screwballs, do you dream? Do you ever dream of the past, Screwballs, of that wintry morning in Bailtefree, and the three days in Bundoran? . . . [*Public stays as he is. Private gets slowly to his feet and moves over to S.B. He stands looking down at him.*]

. . . and of the young, gay girl from beyond the mountains who sometimes cried herself to sleep? [*Softly, nervously, with growing excitement.*] God —maybe—Screwballs—behind those dead eyes and that flat face are there memories of precious moments in the past? My God, have I been unfair to you? Is it possible that you have hoarded in the back of that mind of yours—do you remember—it was an afternoon in May— oh, fifteen years ago—I don't remember every detail but some things are as vivid as can be: the boat was blue and the paint was peeling and there was an empty cigarette packet floating in the water at the bottom between two trout and the left rowlock kept slipping and you had given me your hat and had put your jacket round my shoulders because there had been a shower of rain. And you had the rod in your left hand—I can see the cork nibbled away from the butt of the rod—and maybe we had been chatting—I don't remember—it doesn't matter—but between us at that moment there was this great happiness, this great joy—you must have felt it

89

too—it was so much richer than a content—it was a great, great happiness, and active, bubbling joy—although nothing was being said —just the two of us fishing on a lake on a showery day—and young as I was I felt, I knew, that this was precious, and your hat was soft on the top of my ears—I can feel it—and I shrank down into your coat—and then, then for no reason at all except that you were happy too, you began to sing: [*sings*]

> *All round my hat I'll wear a green coloured*
> > *ribbono,*
>
> *All round my hat for a twelve month and a day.*
> *And if anybody asks me the reason why I wear it,*
> *It's all because my true love is far, far away.*

[*The rosary is over. Madge and S.B. get slowly to their feet. Public and Private are not aware that the prayers are finished. S.B. does the nightly job of winding the clock.*]

MADGE Will you take your supper now?

S.B. Any time suits you.

[*Madge goes to Public, still kneeling.*]

MADGE And what about St. Martin de Porres?

PUBLIC Mm?

[*He blesses himself hurriedly, in confusion, and gets to his feet.*]

MADGE Supper.

PUBLIC Yes—yes—please, Madge——

MADGE [*going off*] I suppose even the saints must eat now and again, too.

[*Pause. S.B. consults his pocket watch.*]

S.B. What time do you make it?

PUBLIC Quarter to ten.

S.B. It's that anyhow.

PRIVATE Go on! Ask him! He must remember!

S.B. The days are shortening already. Before we
know we'll be burning light before closing time.

PRIVATE Go on! Go on!

PUBLIC [*in the churlish, off-hand tone he uses to S.B.*] What
ever happened to that aul boat on Lough na
Cloc Cor.

S.B. What's that?

PRIVATE Again!

PUBLIC That aul boat that used to be up on Lough na
Cloc Cor—an aul blue thing —d'you remember it?

S.B. A boat? Eh? [*Voices off.*] The Canon!

PRIVATE Bugger the Canon!
[*The Canon enters; a lean, white man with alert
eyes and a thin mouth. He is talking back to Madge
in the scullery.*]

CANON Hee-hee-hee—you're a terrible woman.

S.B. Well, Canon!

CANON That Madge . . . hee-hee-hee.

PUBLIC Good night, Canon.

CANON She says I wait till the rosary's over and the
kettle's on . . . hee-hee-hee.

S.B. She's a sharp one, Madge.

CANON 'You wait', says she, 'till the rosary's over and
the kettle's on!'

PRIVATE Hee-hee-hee.

S.B. Pay no heed to Madge, Canon.

PRIVATE And how's the O'Donnell family tonight?

CANON And how's the O'Donnell family tonight?
[*Public sits when the Canon sits.*]

S.B. Living away as usual. Not a thing happening.

PRIVATE Liar!

CANON Just so, now, just so.

S.B. Will we have a game now or will we wait till

91

the supper comes in?

CANON We may as well commence, Sean. I see no reason why we shouldn't commence.

S.B. [*setting the board*] Whatever you say, Canon.

CANON Hee-hee-hee. 'You wait', says she, 'till the rosary's over and the kettle's on.'

PRIVATE She's a sharp one, Madge.

S.B. She's a sharp one, Madge.

CANON It'll be getting near your time, Gareth.

PUBLIC Tomorrow morning, Canon.

CANON Just so, now. Tomorrow morning.

PRIVATE Tomorrow morning.

CANON Tomorrow morning.

S.B. Here we are.

CANON Powerful the way time passes, too.

S.B. Black or white, Canon?

CANON [*considering the problem*] Black or white. . . .

PRIVATE Black for the crows and white for the swans.

CANON Black for the crows and white for the swans.

PRIVATE Ha-ha! [*He preens himself at his skill in prophecy.*]

S.B. Have a shot at the black the night.

CANON Maybe I will then.

PRIVATE Can't take the money off you every night.

CANON Can't take the trousers off you every night. Hee-hee-hee.

PRIVATE [*shocked*] Canon O'Byrne!

S.B. You had a great streak of luck last night, I'll grant you that.

CANON [*a major announcement*] D'you know what?

S.B. What's that, Canon?

CANON You'll have rain before morning.

S.B. D'you think so?

CANON It's in the bones. The leg's giving me the odd jab.

S.B.   We could do without the rain then.

CANON   Before the morning you'll have it.

S.B.   Tch tch tch. We get our fill of it here.

CANON   The best barometer I know.

S.B.   Aye. No want of rain. .

CANON   Before the morning.

S.B.   As if we don't get enough of it.

CANON   The jabs are never wrong.

PRIVATE [*wildly excited*] Stop press! News flash!
        Sensation! We interrupt our programmes to
        bring you the news that Canon Mick O'Byrne,
        of Ballybeg, Ireland, has made the confident
        prediction that *you'll* have rain before the
        morning! Stand by for further bulletins!

CANON   'You wait', says she, 'till the rosary's over and
        the kettle's on!'

S.B.   Usual stakes, Canon?

CANON   I see no reason to alter them.

S.B.   What about putting them up —just for the first
        game?

CANON   The thin end of the wedge, eh, as the Bishop
        says? No, Sean, the way I see it, a half-penny a
        game'll neither make nor break either of us.
        [*Enter Madge with cups of tea and a plate of
        biscuits.*]

MADGE   Have you begun already?

S.B.   Shh!

MADGE   If it was turkeys or marble clocks they were
        playing for they couldn't be more serious!

S.B.   Quiet!

MADGE   Agh!
        [*She leaves their tea beside them and brings a cup
        over to Public. They talk in undertones.*]

MADGE   Wouldn't you love to throw it round them!

PUBLIC   Scalding hot!

MADGE   And raise blisters on their aul bald pates!—God forgive me!

PUBLIC   Madge.

MADGE   What?

PUBLIC   Why don't you take a run over to see the new baby?

MADGE   I've more on my mind than that.

PUBLIC   I'll put up the jars and wash up these few things.

MADGE   And this the last night we'll have you to torment us?

PUBLIC   Go on. Go on. We won't start swopping the dirty stories till we get you out of the road.

S.B.   Shhhhhhh!

PUBLIC   Hurry up. Nelly'll be wondering why you didn't show up.

MADGE   Aye, so.

PUBLIC   Your own namesake, isn't it?

MADGE   So she *says*.

PUBLIC   Get a move on. You'll be back before bedtime.

MADGE   What d'you think?

PUBLIC   Quick!

MADGE   I'm away! [*She takes a few steps away and comes back.*] Don't forget: them shirts isn't right aired. [*Just when she is at the scullery door.*]

PUBLIC   Madge.

MADGE   What is it?

PRIVATE   Don't! Don't!

PUBLIC   Why did my mother marry him [*S.B.*] instead of Master Boyle?

MADGE   What?

PUBLIC   She went with both of them, didn't she?

MADGE   She married the better man by far.

94

PUBLIC But she went with Boyle first, didn't she?

MADGE I've told you before: she went with a dozen—
that was the kind of her—she couldn't help
herself.

PUBLIC But is that what started Boyle drinking?

MADGE If it was, more fool he. And any other nosing
about you want to do, ask the Boss. For you're
not going to pump me.
[She goes off.]

PRIVATE What the hell had you to go and ask that for!
Snap, boy, snap! We want no scenes tonight. Get
up and clear out of this because you're liable to
get over-excited watching these two dare-devils
dicing with death. [Public takes his cup and goes
towards his bedroom.] Into your survival shelter
and brood, brood, brood. [As if replying to the
draught players—who have not noticed his exit.] No,
no, I'm not leaving. Just going in here to have
a wee chat with my Chinese mistress.
[Public goes into his bedroom, leaving the door open.
Private stays in the kitchen. Public in the bedroom
mimes the actions of Private in the following
sequence. Private stands at the table between S.B.
and Canon:]

PRIVATE Canon battling tooth and nail for another
half-penny; Screwballs fighting valiantly to
retain his trousers! Gripped in mortal combat!
County Councillor versus Canon! Screwballs
versus Canonballs! [Stares intently at them.]
Hi, kids! Having fun, kids? [Gets to his feet,
leans his elbow on the table, and talks confidentially
into their faces.] Any chance of a game, huh?
Tell me, boys, strictly between ourselves,
will you miss me? You will? You really will?

95

But now I want you both to close your eyes
—please, my darlings—don't, don't argue—
just do as I say—just close your eyes and
think of all the truly wonderful times we've
had together. Now! What'll we chat about, eh?
Let's —chat—about—what? No, Screwballs, not
women; not before you-know-who. [*Looking at
the Canon.*] Money? Agh, sure, Canon, what
interest have you in money? Sure as long as you
get to Tenerife for five weeks every winter
what interest have you in money? But I'm
wasting my time with you, Canon—Screwballs
here is different; there's an affinity between
Screwballs and me that no one, literally, no one
could understand—except you, Canon [*deadly
serious*], because you're warm and kind and soft and
sympathetic—all things to all men—because you
could translate all this loneliness, this groping,
this dreadful bloody buffoonery into Christian
terms that will make life bearable for us all. And
yet you don't say a word. Why, Canon? Why,
arid Canon? Isn't this your job?—to translate?
Why don't you speak, then? Prudence arid
Canon? Prudence be damned! Christianity isn't
prudent—it's insane! Or maybe this just happens
to be one of your bad nights—[*suddenly bright
and brittle again*]—A pound to a shilling I make
you laugh! [*Dancing around, singing to the tune of
'Daisy':*] 'Screwballs, Screwballs, give me your
answer do. I'm half crazy all for the love of you.
I'm off to Philadelphey, and I'll leave you on
the shelfey——'
[*S.B. gives a short dry laugh.*]
PRIVATE A pound you owe me! Money for aul rope!
96

And you, Canon, what about giving us a bar or
two?

CANON Aye.

PRIVATE You will? Wonderful! What'll it be? A pop
number? An aul Gregorian come-all-ye? A
whack out of an aul aria?

CANON I had you cornered.

PRIVATE 'I had you cornered'—I know it! I know it! I
know it! okay. [*Sings in the style of a modern
crooner.*] I had you cornered/That night in
Casablanca/That night you said you loved me—
all set? Boys and girls, that top, pop recording
star, Kenny O'Byrne and the Ballybeg Buggers
in their latest fabulous release, 'I Had You
Cornered.'
[*Private stands with head lowered, his foot tapping,
his fingers clicking in syncopated rhythm, waiting for
the Canon to begin. He keeps this up for a few
seconds. Then in time to his own beat he sings very
softly, as he goes to the bedroom—*]
> Should aul acquaintance be forgot
> And never brought to min'?
> Should aul acquaintance be forgot
> And days o' lang-syne?
> Yah—ooooo.

[*Public suddenly sits up in bed.*]
Mendelssohn! That's the bugger'll tear the guts
out of you! [*Public puts on a recording of the second
movement of the violin concerto. Private, now almost
frenzied, dashes back to the kitchen.*] Give us a bar
or two, Mendelssohn, aul fella. Come on, lad;
resin the aul bow and spit on your hands and
give us an aul bar!
[*The record begins. Private runs to the table and*

97

thrusts his face between the players.]
Listen! Listen! Listen! D'you hear it? D'you
know what the music says? [*To S.B.*] It says that
once upon a time a boy and his father sat in a
blue boat on a lake on an afternoon in May, and
on that afternoon a great beauty happened, a
beauty that has haunted the boy ever since,
because he wonders now did it really take place
or did he imagine it. There are only the two of
us, he says; each of us is all the other has; and
why can we not even look at each other? Have
pity on us, he says; have goddam pity on every
goddam bloody man jack of us.
[*He comes away from the table and walks limply
back to the bedroom. When he gets to the bedroom
door he turns, surveys the men.*]
To hell with all strong silent men!
[*He goes into the bedroom, drops into the chair, and
sits motionless. Public sinks back on to the bed again.
Silence.*]

CANON   What's that noise?

S.B.   What's that, Canon?

CANON   A noise of some sort.

S.B.   Is there?
       [*They listen.*]

S.B.   I don't hear——

CANON   Wait.

S.B.   Is it——

CANON   It's music—is it?

S.B.   Music?

CANON   Aye. It's music.

S.B.   That'll be Gar then.

CANON   Oh.

S.B.   Playing them records of his.

CANON Thought I heard something.

S.B. All he asks is to sit in there and play them records all day.

CANON It makes him happy.

S.B. Terrible man for the records.

CANON Just so, now. It'll be getting near his time, he tells me.

S.B. Tomorrow morning.

CANON Tomorrow morning.

S.B. Aye, tomorrow morning. Powerful the way time passes, too.

CANON You wait, says she, till the rosary's over and the kettle's on.

S.B. A sharp one, Madge.

CANON Ah-hah. There's hope for you yet.

S.B. I don't know is there.

CANON No. You're not too late yet.

S.B. Maybe . . . maybe. . . .

CANON No, I wouldn't say die yet—not yet I wouldn't.

Slow Curtain

END OF EPISODE THREE, PART I

PART TWO

[*The small hours of the morning. The kitchen is dimly lit. In the kitchen, just outside the bedroom door, are Gar's cases, and lying across them are his coat, his cap, and a large envelope containing his X-ray and visa. The bedroom is in darkness: just enough light to see Public on the bed and Private in the chair. S.B. comes in from the scullery carrying a cup of tea in his hand. He is dressed in long trousers, a vest, a hat, socks. He moves slowly towards the table, sees the cases, goes over to them, touches the coat, goes back towards the table, and sits there, staring at the bedroom door. He coughs. Immediately Private is awake and Public sits up sleepily in bed.*]

PRIVATE   What—what—what's that? [*Relaxing.*] Madge probably. Looking to see is the door bolted.
[*Public gets out of bed and switches on the light. Looks at his watch.*]
You'll not sleep again tonight, laddo.

PUBLIC   Bugger.
[*Public looks at himself in the mirror and then sits on edge of bed.*]

PRIVATE   Four more hours. This is the last time you'll lie in this bed, the last time you'll look at that pattern [*on the floor*], the last time you'll listen to the silence of Ballybeg, the last time you'll——

PUBLIC   Agh, shut up!

100

PRIVATE It is now sixteen or seventeen years since I saw the Queen of France. Go into the shop, man, and get yourself a packet of aspirin; that'll do the trick. [*Looking up at ceiling.*] Mind if I take a packet of aspirin, Screwballs? Send the bill to the U.S.A., okay? Out you go, boy, and get a clatter of pills!
[*They both go into the kitchen. Public stops dead when he sees S.B. staring at him.*]

PRIVATE My God! Lady Godiva!

PUBLIC Is this where you are?

S.B. Aye—I—I—I—I wasn't sleeping. What has you up?
[*Public goes to where the key of the shop is hung up.*]

PUBLIC I—I wasn't sleeping either. I'll get some aspirins inside.

S.B. It's hard to sleep sometimes. . . .

PUBLIC It is, aye . . . sometimes. . . .

S.B. There's tea in the pot.

PUBLIC Aye?

S.B. If it's a headache you have.

PUBLIC It'll make me no worse anyway.
[*Public goes into the scullery. Private stands at the door and talks into him.*]

PRIVATE Now's your time, boy. The small hours of the morning. Put your head on his shoulder and say, 'How's my wee darling Daddy?'
[*Public puts his head round the door.*]

PUBLIC You take some?

S.B. Sure you know I never take a second cup.

PRIVATE Playing hard to get. Come on, bucko; it's your place to make the move—the younger man. Say—say—say—say, 'Screwballs, with two magnificent legs like that, how is it you were

101

never in show biz?' Say, 'It is now sixteen or seventeen——'—Say—oh my God—say—say something.

[*Public enters with a cup of tea.*]

PUBLIC You'll need a new tyre for the van.

S.B. What one's that?

PUBLIC The back left-hand one. I told you. It's done.

S.B. Aye. So you did.

PUBLIC And—and——

PRIVATE What else?

PUBLIC —and don't forget the fencing posts for McGuire next Wednesday.

S.B. Fencing posts.

PUBLIC Twelve dozen. The milk lorry'll take them. I spoke to Packey.

S.B. Aye. . . . right. . . .

PRIVATE Go on! Keep talking!

PUBLIC And if you're looking for the pliers, I threw them into the tea chest under the counter.

S.B. Which tea chest?

PUBLIC The one near the window.

S.B. Oh, I see—I see. . . .

PRIVATE You're doing grand. Keep at it. It's the silence that's the enemy.

PUBLIC You'll be wanting more plug tobacco. The traveller'll be here this week.

S.B. More plug.

PUBLIC It's finished. The last of it went up to Curran's wake.

S.B. I'll—I'll see about that.

PUBLIC And you'll need to put a new clasp on the lower window—the tinkers are about again.

S.B. Aye?

PUBLIC They were in at dinner time. I got some cans off

them.

S.B. I just thought I noticed something shining from the ceiling.

PUBLIC It's the cans then.

S.B. Aye.

PUBLIC That's what it is. I bought six off them.

S.B. They'll not go to loss.

PUBLIC They wanted me to take a dozen but I said six would do us.

S.B. Six is plenty. They don't go as quick as they used to—them cans.

PUBLIC They've all got cookers and ranges and things.

S.B. What's that?

PUBLIC I say they don't buy them now because the open fires are nearly all gone.

S.B. That's it. All cookers and ranges and things these times.

PUBLIC That's why I wouldn't take the dozen.

S.B. You were right, too. Although I mind the time when I got through a couple of dozen a week.

PUBLIC Aye?

S.B. All cans it was then. Maybe you'd sell a kettle at turf-cutting or if there'd be a Yank coming home. . . .
[*Pause.*]

PUBLIC Better get these pills and then try to get a couple of hours sleep——

S.B. You're getting the mail-van to Strabane?
[*Public gives him a quick, watchful look.*]

PUBLIC At a quarter past seven.

S.B. [*awkwardly*] I was listening to the weather forecast there . . . moderate westerly winds and occasional showers, it said.

PUBLIC Aye?

S.B. I was thinking it—it—it—it would be a fair enough day for going up in thon plane.

PUBLIC It should be, then.

S.B. Showers—just like the Canon said. . . . And I was meaning to tell you that you should sit at the back. . . .

PRIVATE It is now sixteen or seventeen years—the longest way round's the shortest way home——

S.B. So *he* was saying, too . . . you know there—if there was an accident or anything—it's the front gets it hardest——

PUBLIC I suppose that's true enough.

S.B. So *he* was saying . . . not that I would know—just that he was saying it there. . . .

PRIVATE [*urgently, rapidly*] Now! Now! He might remember—he might. But if he does, my God, laddo—what if he does?

PUBLIC [*with pretended carelessness*] D'you know what kept coming into my mind the day?

S.B. Eh?

PUBLIC The fishing we used to do on Lough na Cloc Cor.

S.B. [*confused, on guard*] Oh, aye, Lough na Cloc Cor—aye—aye——

PUBLIC We had a throw on it every Sunday during the season.

S.B. That's not the day nor yesterday.

PUBLIC [*more quickly*] There used to be a blue boat on it—d'you remember it?

S.B. Many's the fish we took off that same lake.

PUBLIC D'you remember the blue boat?

S.B. A blue one, eh?

PUBLIC I don't know who owned it. But it was blue. And the paint was peeling.

104

S.B. [*remembering*] I mind a brown one the doctor brought from somewhere up in the——

PUBLIC [*quickly*] It doesn't matter who owned it. It doesn't even matter that it was blue. But d'you remember one afternoon in May—we were up there—the two of us—and it must have rained because you put your jacket round my shoulders and gave me your hat——

S.B. Aye?

PUBLIC —and it wasn't that we were talking or anything —but suddenly—suddenly you sang 'All Round My Hat I'll Wear a Green Coloured Ribbono'——

S.B. Me?

PUBLIC —for no reason at all except that we—that you were happy. D'you remember? D'you remember?

[*There is a pause while S.B. tries to recall.*]

S.B. No . . . no, then, I don't. . . .

[*Private claps his hands in nervous mockery.*]

PRIVATE [*quickly*] There! There! There!

S.B. 'All Round My Hat'? No, I don't think I ever knew that one. It wasn't 'The Flower of Sweet Strabane', was it? That was my song.

PUBLIC It could have been. It doesn't matter.

PRIVATE So now you know: it never happened! Ha-ha-ha-ha-ha.

S.B. 'All Round My Hat'?—that was never one of mine. What does it go like?

PUBLIC I couldn't tell you. I don't know it either.

PRIVATE Ha-ha-ha-ha-ha-ha-ha-ha.

S.B. And you say the boat was blue?

PUBLIC It doesn't matter. Forget it.

S.B. [*justly, reasonably*] There was a brown one

belonging to the doctor, and before that there was a wee flat-bottom—but it was green—or was it white? I'll tell you, you wouldn't be thinking of a punt—it could have been blue—one that the curate had down at the pier last summer——

[*Private's mocking laughter increases. Public rushes quickly into the shop. Private, still mocking, follows.*]

—a fine sturdy wee punt it was, too, and it could well have been the. . . .

[*He sees that he is alone and tails off. Slowly he gets to his feet and goes towards the scullery door. He meets Madge entering. She is dressed in outside clothes. She is very weary.*]

MADGE What has you up?

S.B. Me? Aw, I took medicine and the cramps wouldn't let me sleep. I thought you were in bed?

MADGE I was over at Nelly's. The place was upside down.

S.B. There's nothing wrong, is there?

MADGE Not a thing.

S.B. The baby's strong and healthy?

MADGE Grand—grand.

S.B. That's all that matters.

MADGE They're going to call it Brigid.

S.B. Brigid—that's a grand name . . . Patrick, Brigid, and Colmcille. . . .

[*She takes off her hat and coat. S.B. hesitates.*]

Madge. . . .

MADGE You'll get a cold padding about in yon rig.

S.B. Madge, I'll manage rightly, Madge, eh?

MADGE Surely you will.

S.B. I'll get one of Charley Bonner's boys to do the van on Tuesdays and Thursdays and I'll manage rightly?

MADGE This place is cold. Away off to bed.

S.B. It's not like in the old days when the whole countryside did with me; I needed the help then. But it's different now. I'll manage by myself now. Eh? I'll manage fine, eh?

MADGE Fine.

S.B. D'you mind the trouble we had keeping him at school just after he turned ten. D'you mind nothing would do him but he'd get behind the counter. And he had this wee sailor suit on him this morning——

MADGE A sailor suit? He never had a sailor suit.

S.B. Oh, he had, Madge. Oh, Madge, he had. I can see him, with his shoulders back, and the wee head up straight, and the mouth, aw, man, as set, and says he this morning, I can hear him saying it, says he, 'I'm not going to school. I'm going into my daddy's business'—you know— all important—and, d'you mind, you tried to coax him to go to school, and not a move you could get out of him, and him as manly looking, and this wee sailor suit as smart looking on him, and—and—and at the heel of the hunt I had to go with him myself, the two of us, hand in hand, as happy as larks—we were that happy, Madge—and him dancing and chatting beside me—mind?—you couldn't get a word in edge-ways with all the chatting he used to go through. . . . Maybe, Madge, maybe it's because I could have been his grandfather, eh?

MADGE I don't know.

S.B. I was too old for her, Madge, eh?

MADGE I don't know. They're a new race—a new world.

S.B. [*leaving*] In the wee sailor suit—all the chatting he used to go through. . . . I don't know either. . . .

MADGE [*looking at case*] Tomorrow'll be sore on him [*Gar*]: his heart'll break tomorrow, and all next week, and the week after maybe. . . . Brigid—aye, it's all right—[*Trying out the sound of the name*] Brigid—Biddy—Biddy Mulhern—Brigid Mulhern—aye—like Madge Mulhern doesn't sound right—[*Trying it out*]—Madge Mulhern—Madge Mulhern—I don't know—it's too aul'-fashioned or something. . . . Has he his cap? [*Finds it in the pocket of the coat. Also finds an apple.*] . . . Aye, he has. And an apple, if you don't mind—for all his grief. He'll be all right. That Lizzy one'll look after him well, I suppose, if she can take time off from blatherin'. Garden front and back, and a TV in the house of lords —I'll believe them things when I see them! Never had much time for blatherin' women. . . . [*Remembering.*] An envelope. . . . [*She takes two notes from her pocket, goes to the dresser, and finds an envelope. She puts the money into the envelope, and slips the envelope into the coat pocket.*] That'll get him a cup of tea on the plane. I had put them two pounds by me to get my feet done on the fair day. But I can wait till next month. From what I hear, there's no big dances between now and then. . . . [*She stands looking at the bedroom door.*] So. I think that's everything. . . . [*She raises her hand in a sort of vague*

Benediction, then shuffles towards the scullery.] **When the boss was his [*Gar's*] age, he was the very same as him: leppin, and eejitin' about and actin' the clown; as like as two peas. And when he's [*Gar*] the age the boss is now, he'll turn out just the same. And although I won't be here to see it, you'll find that he's learned nothin' in-between times. That's people for you—they'd put you astray in the head if you thought long enough about them.**

[*Public and Private enter from the shop.*]

PUBLIC You down too? Turning into a night club, this place.

MADGE I'm only getting back.

PUBLIC Well, how's the new Madge?

MADGE Strong and healthy—and that's all that matters.

MADGE Were you and the boss chatting there?

PUBLIC When's the christening?

MADGE Sunday. After last Mass.

PUBLIC Madge Mulhern. Are you proud?

MADGE I'm just tired, son. Very tired.

PUBLIC You're sure there's nothing wrong, Madge?

MADGE If there was something wrong, wouldn't I tell you?

PRIVATE Of course she would. Who else has she?

PUBLIC Did you tell her she's getting an elephant out of my first wages?

MADGE Aye, so. The jars are up?

PUBLIC They are.

MADGE And the dishes washed?

PUBLIC All done.

MADGE I'll give you a call at half-six, then.

PUBLIC Madge—Madge, you'd let me know if—if he

got sick or anything?

MADGE Who else would there be?

PUBLIC Just in case . . . not that it's likely—he'll outlive the whole of us. . . .

MADGE Good night.

PUBLIC Sleep well, Madge.

MADGE Sleep well yourself.

[*Madge goes off. Public and Private watch her shuffle off.*]

PRIVATE Watch her carefully, every movement, every gesture, every little peculiarity: keep the camera whirring; for this is a film you'll run over and over again—Madge Going to Bed On My Last Night At Home. . . . Madge. . . . [*Public and Private go into bedroom.*] God, Boy, why do you have to leave? Why? Why?

PUBLIC I don't know. I—I—I don't know.

Quick Curtain